The Open University

Social sciences: a third level course
Historical data and the social sciences
Units 1-4

The quantitative analysis of historical data

Prepared by Michael Drake

The Open University Press

Front cover: Detail from 'Work' by Ford Madox Brown by permission of the City of Manchester Art Galleries.

Back cover: Extract from a railwayman's record book by permission of the British Railways Board. For reasons of confidentiality, the name and number on this document have been changed.

78596

The Open University Press
Walton Hall Milton Keynes

First published 1974

Copyright © 1974 The Open University

Designed by the Media Development Group of the Open University.

Printed in Great Britain by
COES THE PRINTERS LIMITED
RUSTINGTON SUSSEX

ISBN 0 335 04810 2

907
OPE

0119504

This text forms part of an Open University course. The complete list of units in the course appears at the end of this text.

For general availability of supporting material referred to in this text, please write to the Director of Marketing, The Open University, P.O. Box 81, Walton Hall, Milton Keynes, MK7 6AT.

Further information on Open University courses may be obtained from the Admissions Office, The Open University, P.O. Box 48, Walton Hall, Milton Keynes, MK7 6AB.

1.1

Contents   Block 1   Units 1-4

The quantitative analysis of historical data

Introduction to Units 1–4

Bob Hope (or was it Bing Crosby?) used to tell a story that went something like this: 'There's nothing I wouldn't do for Bing and there's nothing Bing wouldn't do for me. So that's what we do, nothing for each other!' To say that relations between history and the social sciences, like those between Bob and Bing, were all promise and no performance, would undoubtedly be an exaggeration. After all, this course would hardly have been possible without some evidence of cooperation between the various disciplines. Nevertheless the actual practices of traditional historians and social scientists are not as close as some of their protestations might lead one to expect. As for statistics few historians feel at home with much more than the 'mean' and the 'percentage'. When it comes to more advanced measures it has been alleged that in the United States of 1970 only about 'three or four dozen' historians with university posts 'had a knowledge of statistics *through multiple correlation and regression* analysis', economic historians excepted (Swierenga 1970 p xv). And even among social scientists in this country, quantitative methods are more 'honoured in the breach than in the observance' – at least so far as undergraduate teaching is concerned.

What then do we aspire to with *Historical data and the social sciences*? Essentially we are trying to synthesize three distinct intellectual orientations. Each is to be found in the Open University, but is more strongly represented in some parts of it than in others. The first of these is the 'theoretical orientation', familiar enough to students of the Science, Technology and Social Science faculties. The second is the 'literary-subjective orientation', at its strongest within the Arts faculty. The third is the 'quantitative orientation' which stems from, but which is not, of course, confined

'Through' is a useful Americanism meaning 'up to and including'. Put simply this kind of analysis measures the effect of several factors (individually and collectively) on the outcome of a particular event. It is not surprising that not many historians – American or otherwise – have mastered it. We shall not teach the techniques in this course although those of us who are still toddlers, statistically speaking, may get some understanding of them when we have learned to walk. For an example of multiple regression analysis, see the course reader (Drake 1973 pp 259–60).

Figure 1: A model of applied historical studies

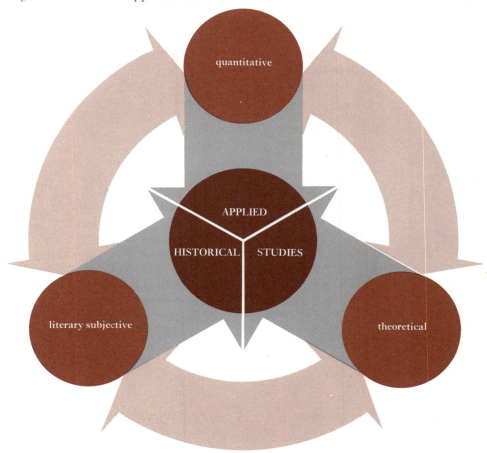

to the faculty of Mathematics. What we understand by each of these so-called 'orientations' is examined in Unit 1. Each will be discussed in a *comparatively elementary fashion*, because each will be presented with one group of students primarily in mind, namely the one least familiar with it. We are also going to try to look at these different orientations in such a way that everyone on the course is conscious of what he is bringing to it as well as being made aware, more frankly perhaps than is often the case, of the suspicion in which his particular 'orientation' is held by others. We hope to dispel the suspicions by discarding the weaknesses and by producing a new synthesis; a true example of inter-disciplinary endeavour where what we end up with is greater than the sum of the contributory parts. And what we end up with, we have called, somewhat pretentiously, *Applied Historical Studies*. It is perhaps pretentious because who are we to stake out a new discipline? On the other hand we have taken the risk because we felt a new label would underline the novelty of the enterprise we are engaged in. In a word, that enterprise is to seek to demonstrate how the development of general laws of human behaviour may in part be facilitated through the statistical manipulation of historical data.

Throughout this block we will be using the literary form as the main vehicle of expression, because we know everyone on the course is literate, but we are fairly certain that numeracy is far from being so widespread. Our evidence for this is mostly impressionistic, but we do have a bit of statistical information. At the end of 1972 about half the students who completed the Social Sciences Foundation Course, *Understanding Society*, were kind enough to complete a questionnaire. One of our questions read: 'All modesty apart, which (if any) of the following are you reasonably competent at? (Indicate as many as you like): i) simple arithmetic, ii) simple graphs, iii) simple algebraic formulas, iv) very elementary statistics (eg mode, median, mean).' Of the 2,300 students completing the questionnaire the numbers admitting to 'reasonable' competence in each of these quantitative techniques were: 2,056; 154; 31 and 46. These figures have been taken by us as the entry behaviour we expect for the numerical part of this course – even though Second Level Courses may, for some students, have raised their numeracy somewhat. Nevertheless we are not shirking the problem. Quantitative techniques are an integral part of Applied Historical Studies. For that reason Units 2–4 are focused upon them.

In preparing any course one has the problem, known variously as hitting the right level, talking the same language or, more grandly, perhaps, providing an appropriate conceptual framework; appropriate, that is, both to the course of study to be undertaken and to the students undertaking it. The difficulty is compounded in the case of this course, partly because it seeks to draw on the three different orientations mentioned above and partly because, like other Open University courses, it can be taken by students whose main work hitherto has been in any one of the University's faculties. It's unlikely then that we shall please 'all of the people all of the time', but perhaps we may succeed in sharing the agony, on the old principle that one man's unit is another man's...!

Unit 1 Words and numbers, sources and theory

Part cover: Nineteenth-century manual workers. Source: Bucks County Record Office, Aylesbury; prison registers 1870-4

Register number: 5826
Occupation: field worker
Age: 64
Marital status: widow
Crime: stole shawl
Sentence: 1 month hard labour

Register number: 5898
Occupation: clerk
Age: 22
Marital status: ?
Crime: stole money
Sentence: 9 months hard labour and 2 years police supervision

Register number: 5488
Occupation: domestic servant
Age: 16
Marital status: ?
Crime: stole a pair of shoes
Sentence: 1 month hard labour

Register number: 5433
Occupation: groom
Age: 30
Marital status: single
Crime: stole a pair of boots
Sentence: 42 days hard labour

Register number: 5891
Occupation: hawker
Age: 79
Marital status: widow
Crime: stole 4 lbs. starch
Sentence: 7 days hard labour

Register number: 5539
Occupation: servant
Age: 20
Marital status: single
Crime: stole money
Sentence: 3 months hard labour

Register number: 4295
Occupation: navvy
Age: 26
Marital status: single
Crime: stole a shirt
Sentence: 21 days hard labour

Register number: 5198
Occupation: domestic servant
Age: 16
Marital status: ?
Crime: stole money from master
Sentence: 1 month hard labour

Register number: 5199
Occupation: housekeeper
Age: 40
Marital status: married
Crime: stole preserved ginger
Sentence: 14 days hard labour

Register number: 5504
Occupation: domestic servant
Age: 20
Marital status: single
Crime: stole a pair of boots
Sentence: 6 weeks hard labour

Register number: 5489
Occupation: housekeeper
Age: 51
Marital status: married, 8 children
Crime: stole wood
Sentence: 10 days hard labour

Register number: 5666
Occupation: hawker
Age: 43
Marital status: widower
Crime: stole purse and money
Sentence: 4 months hard labour

Contents   Unit 1

Objectives

After studying this unit[1] you should be able to:

1 Describe briefly:

  a The main points of difference between traditional history and the social sciences.

  b The value of theory in Applied Historical Studies.

  c The value of statistics in Applied Historical Studies.

  d The value of the traditional skills of the historian for Applied Historical Studies.

*2 List *ten* different kinds of historical data available for exercises in Applied Historical Studies and give illustrations of *five* from the course reader (Drake 1973).

*3 Give *three* arguments in favour of Applied Historical Studies with an illustration of each.

*4 After reviewing your earlier Open University courses select *one* topic, knowledge of which might be enhanced by being subjected to an exercise in Applied Historical Studies.

5 Select from the course reader (Drake 1973) *one* piece of research, or aspect of one, and describe, in summary form, its progress from the original choice of topic to the confirmation, rejection or modification of the hypothesis stage.

*Embraces objectives for Television Programme 1, *The Question Why*.

---

[1] When speaking of objectives I use the term 'unit' in its widest sense to include the correspondence text, associated reading, exercises and relevant television and radio programmes.

Words and numbers, sources and theory

1 The problems of history and the historian

In common everyday language, the word 'history' has two meanings. On the one hand it embraces all that happened in the past; on the other, it refers to accounts of what happened, written by historians (Schiller and Odén 1970 p 17). For our purposes the difference, elementary though it may seem, is rather important. It is so because the distinction between the incalculable number of events of the past and the narrowly limited accounts of them which historians have provided is rarely made explicit; nor is that between the billions of items of data referring to those events and the small range of questions which historians have sought to answer. What, in other words, we are trying to say is that history must not be judged in terms of its practitioners, either when it comes to the data that have been collected, the questions that have been put or the methods of enquiry which have been used to link the two together. I will try now to illustrate the point.

Just over twenty years ago I sat an entrance scholarship examination at one of the Cambridge colleges. One paper was entitled *English History*. There were thirty-one questions: we had to answer four in three hours. Looking over this paper recently I was struck by three things. First, about half the questions concerned named individuals. For example:

Question 2 Compare Lanfranc and Becket.
Question 6 'Both Simon de Montfort and Edward I were splendid failures.' Discuss.
Question 10 In what respects were the Black Prince and John of Gaunt typical of their age?
Question 16 Compare Wolsey and Thomas Cromwell as early Tudor statesmen.
Question 19 'Charles I and Laud were each other's worst enemy.' Discuss.

Secondly, about three-quarters of the questions covered constitutional, governmental or party political matters. In addition to those above there were such questions as:

Question 15 'Henry VII's use of Star Chamber and Privy Council epitomized his new approach to government.' Discuss.
Question 22 Why was it that, down to 1688, so many of the major constitutional conflicts were fought out in the religious field?
Question 29 When, why and in what sense did Gladstone become a Liberal?

The third feature of the paper to strike me was the cliché-ridden style of some of the questions, more appropriate one might think for the saloon bar than for an academic study of human behaviour. Phrases such as 'splendid failures', 'typical of their age' or 'each other's worst enemy' score high marks for neither clarity nor originality.

These points have something in common with those voiced by Herbert Spencer (1820–95), one of the founders of sociology. He wrote:

> ... whether the story of Alfred and the cakes is a fact or a myth, whether Queen Elizabeth intrigued with Essex or not, where Prince Charles hid himself, and what were the details of this battle or the other siege [are] pieces of historical gossip which cannot in the least affect men's conceptions of the ways in which social phenomena hang together ...
> (Spencer 1904, Vol. II, p 265)

This view is still shared by many contemporary social scientists, though it is rarely articulated quite so scathingly. But how far is it justified? So far as *subject matter* is concerned there has been a shift away from the narrow focus on 'major' political figures towards studies of more humble people and also away from the history of individuals to that of groups. At a general level, the rapid growth of economic and social history is one example of this: more parochially, the courses on industrialization and war and society produced by historians of the Open University are another. This broadening of the subject base of history has not, however, led to the rapproche-

The 1972 *British History* paper comparable to the one I took reflects these changes. Unfortunately, a direct comparison is not possible as the Cambridge colleges now have a joint examination (the *British History* paper being a part) 'for men candidates in

ment between historians and social scientists one might have expected. There are several reasons for this.

First, despite the extension in the range of subject matter, there are still many topics of interest to the social scientist that have barely been touched: still a lot of 'answers waiting to be questioned' (Swierenga 1970 p 60).[1] Consequently, a lot of historical data lies undisturbed or has been explored only recently by behavioural historians. Illustrations of this material appear throughout the units of this course, and in the course reader detailed discussions of several are to be found. Take, for instance, the poll-books which are discussed by Nossiter (Drake 1973 pp 251–64). Such books recorded the votes of each individual taking part in parliamentary elections prior to the Act inaugurating the secret ballot in 1872. Nossiter expresses surprise that, as so many poll-books are readily available in print, 'historians have paid so little attention to the study of individual voting behaviour from 1832 to 1871.' Yet the reason is not far to seek. Vincent, whose work on poll-books first brought them to the attention of modern historians, noted in doing so that our 'knowledge of Victorian political behaviour has hitherto been nearly entirely qualitative, not to say anecdotal' (Vincent 1967 p 5). The words to note here are 'qualitative and anecdotal'. We shall return to them later.

History and men and women candidates in Economics'. Of the 49 questions, 11 'concerned named individuals'; 26 'covered constitutional, governmental and party political matters'. As for clichés, there were none. For more on this issue see Unit 2 pp 52, 55–6.

Figure 2 (a): Canvasser's book for 1865 Banbury parliamentary election. Source: Banbury Public Library

1865.

BANBURY AND NEITHROP.

HIGH STREET.

Probably Vote for. 1	2	3	Name of Voter.	How Voted in 1859. February. S.	H.	M.	April. S.	D.	New Voters.
		—	John Gazey			1		1	
—			William Munton	1			1		
—			James Stockton	1			1		
—			Edward Day	1			1		
	—		Robert H. Brooks			1		1	
	—		Richard H. Rolls					1	
	—		Daniel P. Pellatt						1
	—		Joseph Shayler						1
	—		James Hutchings			1		1	
	—	—	James Hall			1		1	
—			George Watson			1			
	—		Richard Fisher			1		1	
		—	George Cottam		1				
—			Thomas Draper	1			1		
—			Thomas Mitchell	1			1		
—			Robert S. Wise.	1			1		
—			Frederick Staines	1			1		
—			William Hobley			1			
		—	Henry W. Clarke						1
			Henry Flowers			1		1	

Figure 2 (b): Poll book of 1832 Aylesbury parliamentary election. Source: Bucks County Record Office, Aylesbury

CANDIDATES.

WILLIAM RICKFORD, Esq.
HENRY HANMER, Esq.
T. B. HOBHOUSE, Esq.

ELECTORS

OF THE

BOROUGH OF AYLESBURY,

Under the 2d William IV. c. 45.

AYLESBURY WITH WALTON.

Names.	*Residence.*	No. in Rgstr.	R.	Han.	Hol
Avery Michael, shoemaker	Walton-street	151	—	—	
Avery Thomas, labourer	Kingsbury	153	—	—	
Ames George, shoemaker	Sharp's-buildings	142	—		—
Avery Sextus, labourer	Hale Leys	152	—		—
Atkins Richard, shoemaker	Castle-street	148	—	—	
Asbury Thomas, hairdresser	Broad-street	146	—		—
Atkins William, huxter	Baker's-lane	150	—		—
Allen James, sweep	Castle-street	141	—	—	
Arnold John, shopkeeper	Kingsbury	145	—		—
Ashfield Charles Robert, clerk	Walton	1	—	—	
Ames Thomas, shoemaker	Temple-street	143	—		—
Archer Rev. Thomas, clerk	Whitchurch	144		—	
Bailey Joseph, basketmaker	Castle-street	154	—		—
Brickland John, cook	Walton-street	180	—	—	
Ballard Joseph, waiter	Behind Bull's Head	159	—	—	
Bradbury Grant, currier	Behind Church	178	—		—
Baldwin Jacob, shoemaker	Back-street	161	—		—
Berry Thomas James, shoemaker	Market-place	170	—	—	

[1] 'What is a collection of historical data but a collection of answers waiting to be questioned? If the questions are unanswerable the answers are unknowable.' Marshall Smelser and William I. Davison, 'The historian and the computer: introduction to complex computation', Swierenga 1970 pp 53–66.

A second reason for the gap between historians and social scientists is that they each ask different questions, and use a somewhat different vocabulary in doing so.[1] Eileen Power (1889–1940), one of this country's leading economic historians, put the point succinctly:

> . . . What, we may ask ourselves, is the true relation between social history and sociology? It must be perfectly plain that a science concerned with the study of man in society must turn to history for one of its most prolific sources of data. Yet if we examine the best works of general sociology we shall discover that the use which they make of historical evidence is comparatively small, and that those chapters in which they deal with it are usually inferior to the chapters in which they deal with anthropological evidence. They draw their best material from contemporary field-work among primitive societies or in *Middletown*, but the space between the *Trobriand Islanders* and Main Street is a howling void, and the whole process of change in time is to a great extent shirked. For this I think the blame must be placed not upon the sociologist, but upon the historian. The former cannot make use of the latter's evidence, because the historian has rarely asked himself the questions to which the sociologist wants an answer. (Eileen Power in Harte 1971 pp 111–12)

Those words were spoken by Professor Power in her inaugural lecture at the London School of Economics as long ago as 1933. There is plenty of evidence, some of it in the course reader, that the situation is still with us today. And the reason too seems to be the same. As she pointed out over forty years ago, 'economic historians . . . have often approached their subject either with no theory at all, or with a theory that is inappropriate to it, a legal, an institutional, or a political theory' (Harte 1971 p 115) and as examples she cited Vinogradoff's studies of the medieval manor as being legal rather than economic or Cunningham's *The Growth of English Industry and Commerce in Modern Times* as more a history of economic policy than an economic history. Some years later T. S. Ashton (1889–1968) reiterated the point when he noted that:

> . . . the very periods into which economic historians divide, one from another, their varied specialisms, are still described in terms drawn from the vocabulary of politics or political history. 'The Feudal System', 'Mercantilism', 'Laissez-Faire', 'Collectivism': the ideas behind words such as these are associated with the policies of government rather than with the postulates of economic science. (Harte 1971 pp 165–6)

A more recent example is furnished by E. G. West. He notes that:

> . . . In many works on nineteenth-century education it is often not made clear that what the author is primarily concerned to record is not so much the development of education as the growth of the centralized political control of it. Since it is easy for the unwary reader to confuse the two, the impression is frequently established without demonstration that 'education did not really start' until it was 'organized', until it became 'public', that is until a particular nineteenth- or twentieth-century Act of Parliament was passed. (Drake 1973 pp 58–9)

In making the point that one of the factors inhibiting the use of history by social scientists (and I use the word history here in both the senses noted above, ie as data and as analysis) is that historians ask the wrong questions, I have also indicated the reason for this. It is that the questions are framed, albeit often unconsciously, in traditional political or legal terms rather than those of contemporary social science. One reason for this is that the historian's *early fare* is still that which produced the sort of questions which, as I mentioned earlier, I attempted to answer some twenty years ago. And it seems to stick. As Stephan Thernstrom has pointed out, historians may say that:

The Trobriand Islanders were a 'primitive' people of the Pacific studied by Bronislaw Malinowski, pioneering what has become known as the 'participant observation' technique. His monographs on them have been described as 'certainly the most formative influence on the work of British social anthropologists from 1922, when he published his first field study, until his death in 1942' (Audrey Richards in Raison 1969 p 188). Equally seminal were the works by Robert S. and Helen M. Lynd on *Middletown* (a pseudonym for the small Indiana town of Muncie). It has been said that they 'set the style for future community studies' and that their work has become 'for the sociologist of the community what Durkheim's *Suicide* is for sociology as a whole' (Bell and Newby 1972 pp 82–3). For a short critical note of the *Middletown* studies see Thernstrom in the course reader (Drake 1973 p 227).

For more on this see Unit 2 pp 52, 55–6.

---

[1] For a fuller discussion of this see the article by Kai T. Erikson, 'Sociology and the historical perspective' in Drake 1973 pp 13–30.

. . . the study of the past enriches the mind and liberalizes the spirit, undermining the instinctive parochial prejudices of those who have been exposed to only one culture, one world-view, one way of life. But it does not follow, I fear, that historians as a breed are conspicuously liberal and open minded in their reception of new methodologies and new research technologies. (Swierenga 1970 pp 67–8)

One should, perhaps, add that it is not only historians who are fixed in their ways. Social scientists too can be equally obtuse. For instance, Thernstrom himself and Stuart Blumin in their respective chapters in the course reader, both upbraid the sociologist for sticking to occupation as a *surrogate* for social class (Drake 1973, especially pp 23c–2 and 234–6).

So far in our analysis of the reasons for the estrangement of historians from social scientists we have looked at two contributory factors: the range of subject matter used by historians and the kind of questions they have asked. So far this has been a somewhat one-sided review: we have not yet examined why historians feel estranged from the social sciences. But before we come to that let us look at a third factor, namely the methods of enquiry used by historians. To sum these up, rather grossly: they are a reliance on qualitative rather than quantitative evidence and a rather naive and casual approach to explanation, which contrasts sharply with the rigorous and sophisticated critique which they apply to their sources. We will take these in turn.

First, the use of qualitative evidence: this stems to a very considerable extent from the fact that history is literature-based. Its practitioners, and subscribers, still place great stress on the literary form, on the elegance of the narrative, in a word, on readability. Numerical paraphernalia such as tables, equations, graphs and models do undoubtedly impede the flow of the narrative. This literary tradition has associated strengths, to which we shall return, but for the moment we will concentrate on its critical weakness. And that is the fact that the cast of mind which makes for a good historian, in terms of his ability to communicate his findings, also leads him to draw upon literary, impressionistic and qualitative rather than quantitative evidence even when the latter is available. It has been argued by one historian that 'it is seldom wise for the historian to dispute what seemed commonsense to contemporaries' (Connell 1951 p 229). Unfortunately, there is plenty of evidence to refute this particular judgement, especially, of course, when one is relying on contemporaries for judgements on essentially quantitative matters. The course reader provides several *illustrations*. For instance, West notes how the Select Committee on Education of the Poorer Classes, which reported in 1838, having 'brushed aside much of the quantitative evidence . . . was impressed by many of the pessimistic qualitative details provided by the local statistical societies' (Drake 1973 p 83).

The burden of his article is that present-day historians of education have done much the same. It is interesting too that Hurt, who vigorously disputes West's interpretation of the condition of British nineteenth-century education, also illustrates how qualitative evidence of quantitative matters can be very unreliable. Commenting on the question of school attendance registers he quotes R. R. W. Lingen, secretary of the Committee of Council on Education. 'No one', notes Lingen, 'would believe, who had not made the experiment, how great is the difference of the result, in averages and other particulars, when taken from general impressions, and when calculated from actual entries' (Drake 1973 p 103). Another example, on a different subject, is given in the course reader. Thernstrom notes that some historians (and sociologists!) writing of social mobility in nineteenth-century America have 'assumed that if contemporary witnesses *thought* that opportunities [of upward social mobility] were declining, they must have been in fact . . .' (Drake 1973 p 223 footnote 7.)

It could be argued that, though contemporaries (and historians relying on them) may be fallible when it comes to the sort of issue detailed above, this is not critical since only a proportion of historical evidence is quantitative. Although this is true,

One definition of 'surrogate measures' is that they are 'measures of something else, not quite what we're after, but perhaps close enough to stand in place of the actual thing until greater insight or better techniques are available'. Abler 1971 p 105 et seq.

Welsh students will perhaps be familiar with a classic example from their own country, namely the evidence appearing in the *Report of the Commissioners of Inquiry into the State of Education in Wales, 1847*. The memory of *brâd y llyfrau gleision* the 'betrayal of the blue books' is apparently still fresh.

"Education is the Systematic Training of the Hand, the Head and the Heart."

Elementary & Middle Class Training Schools,

FOR CHILDREN,

WILKIN STREET, KENTISH TOWN,

NEAR THE NORTH LONDON RAILWAY STATION.

THESE SCHOOLS are designed to provide a thoroughly practical education for the children of respectable families, especially those who object to sending them to the Public Schools, and yet are anxious to have some guarantee for securing more efficient training and better teaching than they can otherwise obtain.

They have been founded and are superintended by a Lady of long experience in educational systems, and the Head Mistress has passed through a course of training, and received credentials of proficiency as an educator of the young.

The following gentlemen kindly give the sanction of their names to the undertaking, thereby affording a sufficient guarantee of the thoroughly Evangelical but undenominational character of the

Annual Grants
FORM NO. III.

N.B. It is particularly requested that the Class, *as well as* the local name of the School, may be specified ; *e.g.*, THORPE NATIONAL SCHOOL ; OATLANDS CHURCH OF ENGLAND SCHOOL (not connected with the National Society) ; BRISTOL, RED CROSS STREET, BRITISH SCHOOL ; &c. The designation given should be *full and distinctive*, and should be written without alteration at the head of every future communication.

England and Wales.

To complete E.I. Report.

good

Hanging Heaton National School

County of *York WRY* 78

Correspondent *Revd Robert Mitchell*

Address *Hanging Heaton*

Post Town *Dewsbury*

Batley

12

PRELIMINARY STATEMENT respecting the Income and Expenditure of the School, in cases where the School has been erected with aid from the Committee of Council.

I. Date of Erection of present School Buildings. *1843*

II. *a.* Condition as to Repair and Ventilation. *good*

b. With what materials are the School-rooms floored? *deal boards*

III. ANNUAL INCOME (*a*) for the Year ending *September 30th* 18*60.*

	Endowment. £ s. d.	Voluntary Contributions. £ s. d.	School Pence. £ s. d.	Other Sources.* £ s. d.	TOTAL. £ s. d.
Boys	5	10	15 0 10		
Girls			17 18 10		
Infants ..					
TOTAL..	5	10	32 19 8		

		Rates of Weekly Payments, and Number of Children paying at each Rate†		
Boys	Rates ..	4ᵈ	3ᵈ	2ᵈ
	Number..	5	14	29
Girls	Rates ..	4	3	2
	Number..	18	12	19
Infants	Rates ..			
	Number..			

Does the School receive any, and, if so, what annual aid from any general and permanent charitable Endowment, such as Betton's Charity ? *— £5 . 0 . 0*

Does the School receive any, and if so, what annual aid from any General Fund arising from annual voluntary Subscriptions or Collections ?

* *Specify* the sources from which this part of the Income is derived.

† What determines the different rates of payment ? *determined according to classes*

(*a*) When the School has not been open **twelve** months, or when from any other cause the actual Income and Expenditure and numbers in attendance paying at different rates cannot be ascertained, an estimate may be given instead.

NOTE.—*Rates of payment may rise according to the means of the parents, or according as a child passes from the lower to the upper classes in a School. The highest class in a School should be accessible for a fee fairly within the means of a common labouring man in the neighbourhood. Scales of payment simply varying* PER SUBJECT TAUGHT *cannot be approved, as they make the classification of a School dependent upon other causes than the proficiency of the Scholars.*

IV. ANNUAL EXPENDITURE (*a*) for the Year ending *September 30* 1860.

	Salary of † Teacher.	Salary of Assistants.	Books and Apparatus.	Fuel and Lights.	Repairs.	Rent.	Other Expenses.	TOTAL.	Cost per Child.
Boys	47 19 8		1 10 0	1 1	4 10 0	5	3 10 0	58 15 8	15 8
Girls									
Infants									
TOTAL..									

† *This should include the whole Amount received by the Teacher for his (or her) own use, whether consisting of School Pence, fixed Stipend, or a Grant from some General Fund, but* NOT *any Sums awarded by the Committee of Council.*

Are the Teachers, or any of them, provided by the Managers with houses or suitable lodgings rent-free, in addition to the above salary ? What is the number of rooms in each house ? *No*

V. *a.* How is the deficiency (if any) supplied ?

b. Are there any debts affecting the Schools beyond those of the current year ?

it does seem to be the case that many historians have failed to recognize just how big this proportion is. This is because many of the assessments used by historians, and many of the statements made by them in turn, are *implicitly* quantitative. As Schofield has put it, 'many apparently literary statements in history are covertly quantitative. Non-numerical, even anti-numerical historians who use words such as "common", "negligible", "intense", "growing", and "stable" are making quantitative statements and they should expect them to be evaluated according to the rules of quantitative argument' (Schofield 1972 p 326). To close this section, let me quote the rather severe comment of Fogel:

> . . . authoritative opinions of the past, on most quantitative matters which concern economic historians, are crude approximations derived from poor data on the basis of inadequate statistical tools. They should not be accepted without statistical verification unless the absence of data makes verification impossible. (Fogel 1964 p 245)

We turn now to explanation in history. The charge has been made that, whereas historians exercise scrupulous care in ascertaining whether or not an event has taken place, they are very amateurish when it comes to explaining it (Hughes 1960 p 21). The point is not a new one; it was made thirty years earlier by R. H. Tawney (1880–1962).

> For one thing, historians, with certain conspicuous exceptions, have continued to employ unanalysed concepts – nation, state, political power, property, progress, commercial supremacy, and a host of similar clichés – with an exasperating naivety. If critical in their use of sources, they have been astonishingly uncritical of the conceptions employed to interpret the data derived from them. Such scrupulousness as to facts and casualness as to categories is as though a judge should be a master of the law of evidence, and then base his decisions on the juristic notions of the tenth century. For another thing, with certain brilliant exceptions, they have preferred burrowing to climbing. They make a darkness, and call it research, while shrinking from the light of general ideas which alone can illuminate it. In the third place, the narrative form which descends from the chronicle, and which is still the commonest method of organizing historical material, is not adequate to a large range of problems facing the historian today . . . it is too simple a procedure to reveal effectively the relations between different elements in a complex situation . . . (Harte 1971 p 105).

Examples of this naivety are to be found in the questions from the Cambridge examination paper that I cited earlier. I would like to quote one other example. It is *not* from the work of a historian but it does, I think, encapsulate, in an extreme form, the kind of *post hoc* reasoning which some historians are prone to. The extract comes from the recent biography of Edward Heath by Margaret Laing.

> . . . Compared with his two immediate predecessors in the Conservative Party – Harold Macmillan, who was born into an upper-middle-class family engaged in publishing, and Alec Douglas-Home, whose family were not only aristocratic but rich – he [Edward Heath] seems at first sight to have had few advantages. In fact, it was to turn out that these very lacks and hardships themselves were in his favour; they nurtured the iron in his temperament and gave it a cutting edge in maturity.
> He also had one unseen advantage. Instead of a nanny he had a mother. Instead of being a small cog in a nursery, he was at the heart of the household, adored by both his parents. (Laing 1972 in *Sunday Times*, 8 October 1972 p 33)

Our criticism so far of the historian's craft has reflected the views of the social scientist as to what constitutes the proper study of man's behaviour in society. We have argued that the historian's chief deficiencies are his focus on a limited range of subject matter, with its corollary, a restricted range of sources; a non-quantitative approach both as regards the sources he uses and the form in which he transmits his findings; and, thirdly, a method of explanation and interpretation owing much to intuition and little to explicit theory. The question of subject matter and data will emerge as the course progresses, and, as a preliminary statement appears in the introduction to the course reader (Drake 1973 pp 2–8), no more will be said about it here. We will, however, examine the other two criticisms, that of explanation and that of numeracy. Erstwhile historians will be relieved to find that so far as their traditional skills are concerned, all is not lost!

2   The promise of theory

When a social scientist talks about explanation he talks about theories. A *theory* is 'an explanation of data phrased with such care that we can test the validity of the explanation itself with another set of data' (Sherif and Sherif 1969 p 62). A *hypothesis* is usually taken to be a provisional explanation, a sort of tentative theory which requires further testing. As it happens the words are used rather loosely by social scientists, particularly sociologists (Weeks 1972 p 67). An interesting example of this is to be found on page 155 of the course reader, where Krause appears to use the two interchangeably. So far as Applied Historical Studies are concerned, theory fulfils three functions. One of these is to improve the quality of description. For instance, take the passage quoted above from Margaret Laing's biography of Edward Heath. Her 'heads I win, tails you lose' technique of accounting for Heath's success in life is based on two mutually contradictory and implicit theories of the effect of upbringing on success in later life. Our objection is that the theories are implicit, that no attempt is made to resolve the contradiction and that as a result this description of part of Heath's upbringing lacks conviction. As it happens this particular area of enquiry (ie child rearing) abounds with difficulties and though much work has been done, what theories there are might more properly be termed hypotheses. (See Crawley and Corcoran 1971 pp 45–8.) Another example of theory improving the quality of description appears in the second television programme for this course. In this we are trying to describe the fluctuations in the number of baptisms recorded in Norway between 1735 and 1865. The details of this 'time series' do not concern us here (for a definition of a 'time series' see Floud 1973 p 85). What does concern us is that statistical theory helps us to dissect the ups and downs of the series into three parts: the long term trend, a more or less regular cycle of about thirty-three years duration and, finally, the irregular fluctuation about the cycle and the trend. Once we have done this we can begin to try to explain the fluctuations.

A second use of theory is that it helps us to formulate questions. (Several examples of this appear in the course reader.) This is hardly surprising since one of the features of Applied Historical Studies is to test the theories derived from contemporary data against the historical record. It follows that the questions to be asked of that record will stem from the theories of today. Take for example the work on social mobility reported by Thernstrom and Blumin (Drake 1973 pp 221–49). They begin by presenting the 'blocked mobility' thesis, namely that in the United States, upward social mobility is more difficult to achieve in the twentieth century than it was in the nineteenth. From this they derive a whole series of questions ranging from the adequacy or otherwise of the time period involved; the basis of the assertions about the rate of upward social mobility in the nineteenth century; the novelty of the thesis; the adequacy of the concept of social mobility; the validity of inferring social mobility from occupational mobility, and many more. In the end by drawing on the historical record, by applying onto contemporary data some of the insights that record provided, Thernstrom and Blumin radically transform the discussion of social mobility, whether that be in the present time or in the past.

Another example in the reader is the use Fogel makes of the *theory of rent*. This is a little more difficult to follow than the Thernstrom-Blumin example, because the theory is not articulated quite so clearly. And in any case, Fogel's whole approach to the problems of explanation is novel. Suffice it to say at this point, Fogel tries to find

'Rent' is not to be confused here with the sum one pays for a house one occupies or a piece of land one uses over a specific period of time. Rather, it is that sum over

what land could feasibly have been farmed in the United States, had there been no railways.

> Without railroads the high cost of wagon transport would have limited commercial agricultural production to areas of land lying within some unknown distance of navigable waterways. It is possible to use the theory of rent to establish these boundaries of feasible commercial agriculture in a non-rail society. Rent is a measure of the amount by which the return to labour and capital on a given portion of land exceeds the return the same factors could earn if they were employed at the intensive or extensive margins. Therefore any plot of land capable of commanding a rent will be kept in productive activity. It follows that, even in the face of increased transport costs, a given area of farm land will remain in use as long as the increased costs incurred during a given time period do not exceed the original rental value of that land. (Drake 1973 p 124)

Armed with this theory, which incidentally, like much economic theory, is deductively rather than inductively derived, Fogel is pointed in the direction of the questions he needs to ask if he is to find the feasible area of agriculture.

> ... Given information on the quantity of goods shipped between farms and their markets, the distances from farms to rail and water shipping points, the distances from such shipping points to markets, and the wagon, rail and water rates, it is possible to compute the additional transport costs that would have been incurred if farmers had attempted to duplicate their actual shipping pattern without railroads. (Drake 1973 p 124)

In 'Von Thünen in retrospect' Andreas Grötewald says that:

> ... rent ... can be explained most easily by a history of settlement ...
>   When [a settlement] was small, only a little land around the city was needed to supply it with agricultural products. As settlement expanded and the demand for agricultural products increased, land at a greater distance had to be taken under cultivation. As a

and above the earnings required to keep a particular factor of production (ie land, labour or capital) employed in its present manner. For example, as a professor I earn a certain amount of money – an excessive amount in some people's eyes. And undoubtedly it is excessive in that I would be prepared to work for less (how much less I'd better keep secret). The difference between what I now earn and that figure which would just be sufficient to keep me as a professor at the Open University is my economic rent. Fogel is applying the concept to American farmland, but the principle is the same.

Figure 5 Area of feasible commercial agriculture, in the absence of railways, in the USA (1890). Source: Fogel (1964, Figure 3.4)

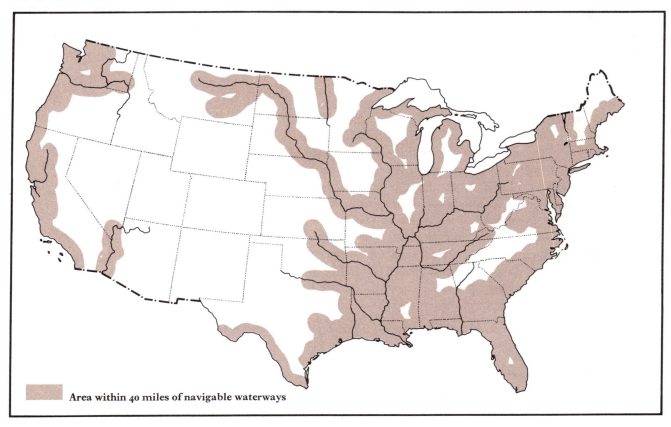

Area within 40 miles of navigable waterways

result of the increased cost of shipping from this outer zone to the city, market prices for agricultural products had to increase. Farmers in the earlier settled area benefited from such higher prices. Compared to farmers in the more recently settled outer zone, they obtained the differential advantage of lower transportation costs to the market; thus their land provided a rent and increased in desirability and value. Eventually, settlement expanded still further and a third zone, even more remote from the city, was taken under cultivation. At this stage, prices for agricultural products in the city had to increase even further. Consequently, the second zone of settlement began to provide a land rent, and in the first settled area the rent increased.

The formula given below indicates how land rent for any one product can be derived:

$$R = Yp - E - Yf\,k$$

In this formula, R = land rent per acre; E = production expenses per acre, including labour, supplies and equipment; Y = yield in units of commodity per acre; p = market price per unit of commodity; f = freight rate, i.e. the cost of shipping a unit of commodity over the distance of one mile; and k = number of miles from the market. (Social Sciences Foundation Course Team pp 289–90)

A third and final value of theory is that it helps us establish laws of human behaviour. For our purposes we will define a 'law' as being towards one end of a spectrum which has a 'hypothesis' at its other end and a 'theory' in the middle. It is, in other words, a somewhat more firmly based explanation of a set of phenomena than is a theory and considerably more so than a hypothesis. Such laws, of course, are not ultimate truths, capable of universal application. But they are of value nonetheless. To quote Eileen Power again:

... No one in his senses has ever pretended that the laws obtainable by the social scientist from the investigation of social reality can be as logically satisfactory as the formal laws of the deductive sciences, or even as those of the physical sciences. Both material and investigator are subject to disadvantages which do not exist in the case of the other sciences. But I conceive the whole trend of modern sociological thought to be in support of the view that it is possible to analyse social behaviour into a certain number of universal abstract relations; and if such laws are no more than rough approximations, that is already a great deal. (Harte 1971 p 118)

Theory is then a powerful weapon but, like all weapons, in the wrong hands it can have disastrous effects. And it is here, I think, that the traditional skills of the historian may act as a safeguard. First, although historians often make implicit generalizations, they are suspicious of formal generalizations, particularly those expressed as 'laws' of human behaviour. Their training attunes them to noting the unique features of every situation. They are, therefore, skilled in seeing situations in all their complexity and quick to spot any attempt to do violence to the facts. A recent attempt to apply psycho-analytical theory to the 'facts' of Hitler's childhood (Langer 1973) has had a rough reception from some historians for this reason. Thus although one needs some kind of filter, some kind of net which will collect the 'facts' one can use and reject those that are irrelevant, and although it is theory (whether recognized explicitly or not) which provides this, there is always the danger of choosing a net with the wrong mesh. Thernstrom in the course reader gives an example of this. Referring to the drawbacks of drawing up a table showing 'the rate of inter-generational movement between manual and non-manual occupations in America since 1700', he notes:

... The concept of social mobility, after all, is an exceptionally rich and complex one, and simple one-dimensional indices which facilitate immediate comparisons of social mobility in radically different social orders may not yield the most rewarding comparisons. The alluring comparability attained by passing disparate sets of data through a sieve so crude that it allows essential features of each set to trickle away is purchased at a very heavy price. (Drake 1973 p 231)

A second way in which the historian may help in the application of theory to historical data arises from his traditional preoccupation with source criticism. We have already noted this particular skill; some, rather cruelly, might say that sometimes it appears to be the be-all and end-all of his discipline. Undoubtedly, however, historians are expected to be particularly concerned with the *reliability* of the evidence they use. The course reader provides an interesting example of a conflict between an economist (E. G. West) and a historian (J. S. Hurt) arising from this very issue. West, trying out 'new theory in the context of old data' (p 53), is countered by Hurt for showing 'remarkable faith in the accuracy of the educational statistics [West's main source of data] that were collected in the first half of the nineteenth century. This faith was shared neither by those by whom they were compiled nor by those for whom they were produced' (p 93).

Finally, it is worth noting that although we have suggested that theory helps us formulate worthwhile questions, it is not the only source of such questions and in some ways may restrict the range of questions and maybe bias the outcome of any enquiry dependent upon them. Historians have a role to play here also. The study of history, taking place, as it so often does, within a humanistic and imaginative tradition, does develop the power of speculation. Untrammelled by the need to 'prove' his conclusions, since in any case he often believes such 'proof' impossible, the historian, 'unsure of his data' as Erikson remarked, 'is invited by the conventions of his trade to fill in the missing information with a fairly deliberate exercise of sympathy and intuition' (Drake 1973 p 22). It is possible that 'history . . . can lead social science itself along the path of imagination and bold hypothesis' (Hughes 1960 p 47).

Students of D281 *New Trends in Geography* may care to turn to pp 48–9 of Unit 14 of that course where Dr Mills talks about the historical geographer's care over source material in rather the same vein.

3   Why do we need statistics?

Statistics, like history, has a double meaning. On the one hand statistics are numbers that represent certain phenomena, eg officially published statistics of imports or exports. On the other hand by statistics we mean the methods used to collect, describe and analyse such numbers (Schiller and Odén 1970 pp 17–18). Again, as with history, the distinction is important. For in order to be able to determine the value of statistics (as numbers) we need to know something of statistics (as methods).

Social scientists use many quantitative concepts which need quantitative terms if they are to have meaning (Blumin in Drake 1973 p 234). Numbers too give precision and accuracy – when properly arrived at. They are valuable too in guiding us to the questions we should ask of our material. For instance, in the television programme I mentioned earlier about the fluctuations in baptisms recorded in Norway between 1735 and 1865, we use statistical techniques to dissect the series into a number of parts, to help us determine what aspects of the series we should focus our attention upon so as to be able to *begin* the task of explaining those fluctuations. For another example, one need only turn to Fogel's article in the course reader.

Our prime justification for using statistics is, however, that which my colleague, Norman Gower, has given as the justification for mathematics as a whole, namely that it helps us to express our ideas on the 'relations between sets of objects'; it guides us in our 'search for pattern and form', it helps us determine 'the structure of things' and it facilitates the search for 'abstraction' (Gower 1973).

There are, as one might expect, drawbacks to the use of quantitative methods. Not all subjects we are interested in can benefit from them (Floud 1973 pp 3–4). Also statistical techniques usually give us approximations, averages, probabilities. The apparent exactness of the number may then lead to a specious confidence in its applicability to *all* cases. Even when this particular trap is avoided it is sometimes not recognized that statistics can be variously interpreted. There are a number of examples of this in the course reader. For instance, Fogel notes that between 1871 and 1890 the railways consumed, annually, somewhere between 50 per cent and

87 per cent of the total output of the American steel industry. This would seem to suggest that the railways played an indispensable role in stimulating the growth of the steel industry. Yet, as Fogel points out, 'there is another way of looking at the data'. This is to look at the time it took for 'non-rail consumption of steel to exceed the total production of a given year'. Because steel production was growing so fast (from 82,000 tons in 1871 to 4,790,000 tons in 1890) this period was only between two and nine years, with an average of six years (Drake 1973 p 135). For instance, in 1875 non-rail consumption of steel was 105,000 tons; yet just four years before, total production of steel had been only 82,000 tons. For another example of the same kind of dual interpretation of the same statistics, though one where the two interpretations are not equally valid as in the Fogel case, see the course reader, pages 101–2 and 114.

The contribution of the historian's skills to the use of quantitative methods is, first, that of evaluating the context which has provided the numerical material and secondly, of attempting in some way to marry the language of words and the language of numbers. Several examples of the first of these roles are given in the course Reader. Hurt's article, for instance, is a very salutary reminder of the need to know one's sources, in this case the educational statistics of early nineteenth-century Britain. Another example is that of Krause who in his article 'Some implications of recent work in historical demography' devotes a considerable amount of attention to the statistical sources used by him and his historical demographer colleagues. One brief example (it appears in a footnote) will suffice to indicate the importance of this task. Krause, commenting on an article by McKeown and Brown, observes that their belief that falling mortality, as a result of environmental improvements, caused the population

Figure 6 The growth of London, 1690–1785. Source: George Rudé (1971) *Hanoverian London, 1714–1808*, London, Secker and Warburg

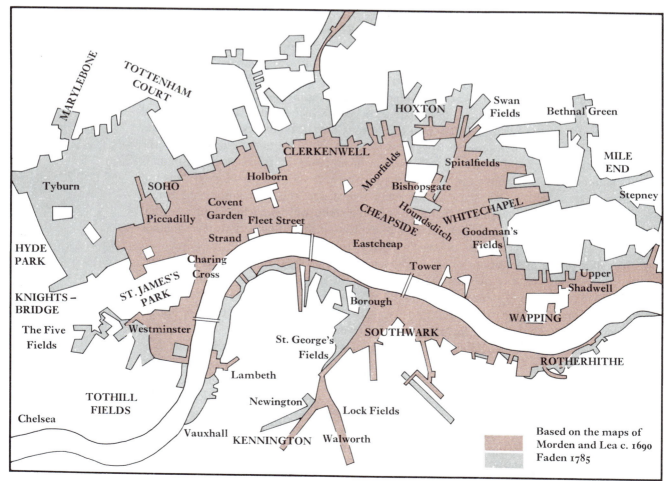

of England to grow in the eighteenth century, drew on some statistics for support. These were 'mainly for London'. Krause then remarks:

> . . . the statistics refer to burials in London, not to deaths of Londoners. As the city increased in size during the century, burial space became increasingly expensive and many cheap burial grounds opened outside the city. More and more burials, especially of the lower classes, occurred outside the limits of the Bills of Mortality [the name given to the registration system]; hence, a large part of the seeming decline of London's mortality during the eighteenth century is explained on the basis of the deteriorating registration of deaths. (Drake 1973 pp 164–5, footnote 23)

As for the language question, the advent of statistics does create a problem of communication. One historian, Professor F. J. Fisher, has remarked that so far as economic history is concerned, 'the history of the nineteenth century is full of every sort of figure except the human' (Harte 1971 p 186). If such is really the case then the traditional audience of the historian is likely to disappear. Nor can one see the Nobel Prize for Literature going to C. Horace Hamilton, if the title of his work – '[The] addition theorem and analysis of variance in the case of correlated nominal variates' – is indicative of the language of its contents! (See Drake 1973 p 245, footnote 18.) Yet statistics, to coin a phrase, are too important to be left to the statistician, or the social scientist. It is hoped that students of Applied Historical Studies will help build a bridge between the literary and the numerical traditions, producing a new frame of mind able to encompass both.

4 Applied Historical Studies: a synthesis

We began this unit by trying to show how historians have gone about their task of understanding the past. We pointed to what we considered some of the limitations of historians as regards both the scope and the methods of their enquiries. We then went on to suggest that the use of explicit theory and statistical techniques would help to improve the quality of description and explanation. One point we have not stressed, though it is implicit in much that we have said and is discussed in the introduction to the course Reader, is that the use of theory and quantitative techniques greatly extends the range of the historical data we can use. This is important, because without this kind of data we would be in no position to develop those general laws of human behaviour, which, as we have said, is the goal of Applied Historical Studies. Such data is, of course, group data – the electoral, demographic, educational, economic activities of *groups* of people – and such laws help us to predict the behaviour of groups in these various matters. The laws of social science do not allow us to predict with much certainty the likely behaviour of a particular individual, but so far as groups are concerned they are much more promising. For instance no social scientist would have been prepared to put much money on the prediction that in 1971 Mr William Walker, 45-year-old sheet metal worker of Wigan would, or would not, elect to read the Social Sciences Foundation Course at the Open University. But had you asked any sociologist of education to take bets on the likely proportion of working-class applicants to the University in that year, you would not have been short of takers – and their predictions would have been close to the observed pattern.

Confusion on this point has persisted for a long time and is still a frequent bone of contention between historians and social scientists. Herbert Spencer summed up the point in his usual blunt way – the historians, in his eyes at least, being the obtuse ones.

> . . . The possibility of Sociology was not only not conceived by historians, but when alleged was denied. Occupied as they had all along been in narrating the *events* in the lives of societies, they had paid little or no attention to the evolution of their organizations. If a biographer, seeing that the incidents of his hero's life did not admit of scientific prevision, therefore said that there is no science of Man, ignoring all the phenomena of bodily formation and function, he would parallel the ordinary historian who, thinking of little

else but the doings of kings, court-intrigues, international quarrels, victories and defeats, concerning all of which no definite forecasts are possible, asserts that there is no social science: overlooking the mutually-dependent structures which have been quietly unfolding while the transactions he writes about have been taking place. (Spencer 1904 Vol II p 253)

Although Herbert Spencer had little time for the historians of his day, as our two quotations from his *Autobiography* have indicated, we have been at pains to point up the valuable contribution historians can make to Applied Historical Studies. We have noted in particular their sensitivity to the uniqueness of situations, their literary gifts, imaginative power, and above all, their attention to the credibility of source material. We need to draw on these skills and to synthesize them with those of the theoretician and the statistician in such a way as to develop the strengths and reduce the weaknesses of all three. Our diagram (Figure 7) purports to show such a synthesis in readily understandable form. But what can we do with our new hybrid? Is it, as

Figure 7 Applied historical studies: static

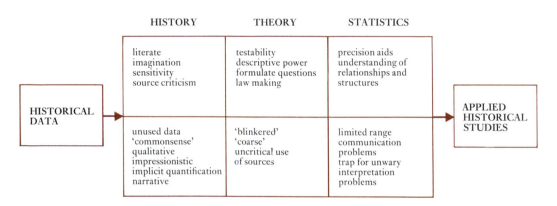

someone has said about interdisciplinary studies in general, rather like that 'supreme achievement of hybridization in the animal world, the mule – a creature without pride of ancestry or hope of progeny'? (Swierenga 1970 p 52). Only you, with your forthcoming projects, will be able to determine the progeny question and only you, at the end of the first half of the course can decide the question of ancestry. However, having outlined the nature of the synthesis, we now need to give it a dynamic, to indicate how the various parts may contribute to our enquiries; in a word provide us with a *research strategy*.

This we have done in diagrammatic form in Figure 8. To illustrate Figure 8 we will fill the boxes from material in Thernstrom's article in the course reader (Drake 1973 pp 221–32).

Figure 8 Applied historical studies: dynamic

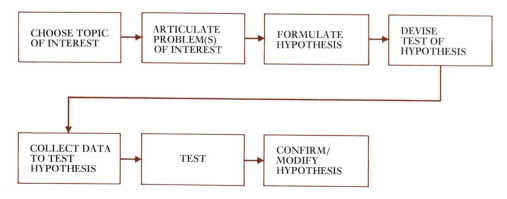

1	**Topic of interest**	– Social mobility.
2	**Articulate problem**	– Has there been any change in rate of upward social mobility in the last 100 years in USA?
3	**Formulate hypothesis**	– Industrialization has reduced rate of upward social mobility in USA over last 100 years.
4	**Devise test**	– Examine number of sons of labourers who moved into white collar jobs at different times over the last 100 years in USA.
5	**Collect data**	– Federal census records.
6	**Test**	– Devise a measure so that comparison of rates of mobility is possible.
7	**Result**	– Hypothesis that industrialization has reduced upward social mobility in USA over the last 100 years not confirmed.

You will notice that this bare statement of Thernstrom's work does little justice to it. Indeed, if we take his work together with that reported by Blumin in the course reader, the skeletal quality of the summary we've just given is even more apparent. For they both raise new questions, explore new leads, which together cause us to re-examine the contents of each of the boxes shown in Figure 8. For instance, as we have already noted (above p 18) they query the adequacy of the concept of 'social mobility'; they demonstrate, as a result of their historical enquiries, the incorrectness of the assumptions which underpinned the modern sociological work on social mobility in the United States and they devise new quantitative measures in order to get closer to economic mobility. Thus in pursuing what appeared to be a relatively straightforward piece of research they opened up a whole new field of enquiry. It is no exaggeration to say that the study of social mobility will never be the same again, in the sense that the foundation on which it was based has been shattered.

Going through the course reader you will come across further examples of this. You yourself when developing your project may well provide others.

Self-assessment questions

SAQ 1 The following quotation comes from an American sociology text-book (Wilson 1966 p 18). The gaps indicate where I have left out the words history/historical and sociology/sociological. Perhaps you might try to fill them in?

... We commonly think of (a)................... as the chronological record of important past events. To distinguish roughly between sociology and history, Bierstedt [Robert Bierstedt 1957 *The Social Order*, New York, McGraw-Hill, pp 8–9] has suggested that (b)................... is 'a particularizing or individualizing discipline [whereas (c)................... is] a generalizing one. (d)................... is a descriptive discipline; (e)................... an analytical one.' Again, it has been suggested that (f)................... typically deals with men and events who ride the crest of the wave, while (g)................... is concerned with the underlying currents of which the dramatic and visible figures are ephemeral symbols. Finally, a distinction has sometimes been made between the words *important* and *crucial*, the former referring to the (h)................... focus, the latter to the (i)................... orientation. (j)................... is concerned with those events necessary (though seldom if ever sufficient) to produce a given outcome. They are, therefore, crucial. On the other hand, (k)................... is preoccupied with events which loom large in the public consciousness, whether or not they are necessary antecedents for certain outcomes.

None of these distinctions is totally true. At most they represent differing emphases. It is easy to cite historians whose investigations resemble sociologists'; and sociologists whose enquiries are barely distinguishable from those of historians.

SAQ 2 Aydelotte has drawn a distinction between two kinds of intellectual activity, both necessary for successful enquiry. The one is 'the means by which we arrive at or formulate a proposition'; the other is 'the means by which, once having obtained it, we attempt to assess its merits'. (William O. Aydelotte, 'Notes on the problems of historical generalization' in Gottschalk 1963 p 166)

Which of the intellectual orientations discussed in the unit would you think might contribute most to these two activities?

SAQ 3 What feature of research method do West and Fogel have in common, judging by their articles in the course reader? Try to select crucial passages which bring out this common element.

SAQ 4 Below are three extracts from West's first article in the course reader. We can take them at their face value or we can try to assess their credibility. Which would you do? If you feel we cannot accept them at their face value, say why not and rank them in order of reliability.

> a . . . Even around London, in a circle of fifty miles, which is far from the most instructed and virtuous part of the kingdom, there is hardly a village that has not something of a school; and not many children of either sex who are not taught, more or less, reading and writing. We have met with families in which, for weeks together, not an article of sustenance but potatoes had been used; yet for every child the hard-earned sum was provided to send them to school (from *Edinburgh Review*, February 1813 cited by West in Drake 1973 p 66).
>
> b . . . The reliance upon Sunday schools was particularly heavy; in Manchester, Kay observed: 'The Report of the Statistical Society shows that the education provided for the poorer classes in Sunday schools is considerably more extensive than in the day schools'. (West in Drake 1973 pp 72–3)
>
> c . . . In the textile town of Pendleton in 1838, 37 out of 2,466 children under ten years (ie 1½ per cent) were found at work. (West in Drake 1973 p 70)

SAQ 5 On page 25 of the unit I used Thernstrom's article in the course reader to illustrate my Figure 8. Turn now to the first article by Krause in the reader (pp 155–83) and do the same exercise.

Answers to SAQs

Answer SAQ 1
(a) history	(g) sociology
(b) history	(h) historical
(c) sociology	(i) sociological
(d) history	(j) sociology
(e) sociology	(k) history
(f) history	

Answer SAQ 2 The obvious answer, I suppose, would be the 'literary subjective' orientation for formulating propositions and the 'quantitative' orientation for testing them. A moment or two's reflection, and perhaps a re-reading of the unit and relevant parts of the course reader, might well suggest, however, that each orientation could contribute to both the formulating and assessment functions. For example in Television Programme 2, as noted above, we use statistical techniques to isolate the trend and the cyclical and non-cyclical fluctuations in Norwegian baptisms over the years 1735–1865. We do this in order to pinpoint particular years of exceedingly high mortality *prior* to asking questions about them. Again, as is made clear in the unit, statistics themselves have to be interpreted and intuition and imagination play a role here. Theory too is important in helping us both to formulate questions and to put them to the test. Nevertheless, it is worth keeping Aydelotte's distinction in mind because it helps us avoid a certain ambiguity. As he points out, in attacking each other, proponents of quantification and rigorous explanatory methods 'may be thinking of the second stage, verification'; whilst proponents of speculation and intuition 'may be thinking of the first stage, getting ideas rather than testing or confirming them'.

Answer SAQ 3 Both West and Fogel adopt what has been called a 'counterfactual' approach. The method is carried to greater lengths by Fogel but nevertheless it is easily identifiable in West's work. In essence the use of the counterfactual method is akin to the 'if' questions which, formally at least, traditional historians have always deplored. In fact, a large number of statements by historians, or all of us for that matter, involve a counterfactual element. For instance, if one states that something or other is 'important', one is by *implication* setting up an alternative situation in which that particular thing is either absent, or playing a lesser role; in other words one is being counterfactual. Both West and Fogel argue that by failing to recognize this in various situations we have distorted our view of past events, and, of course, continue to do so about current ones as well. The quotations from the course reader which I think bring this out are as follows:

> . . . The Britain of the nineteenth century was, as everyone knows, littered with such external effects [as 'congestion, noise, smell, smoke, health-risk, ugliness, and ignorance']. The historian's mere act of documenting them, nevertheless, does not prove past resource misallocation. (West in Drake 1973 p 55)
> . . . No one believes, for instance, that because it is only now in the twentieth century that legislative attempts are being made to weld transport into 'one co-ordinated system of public transport' that transport did not seriously exist or make any progress in the nineteenth century. So long as histories of education continue to be written predominantly in terms of the chronological sequence of legislation, many readers must certainly be forgiven for deriving the impression of an implicit presumption that no substantial progress could have occurred without it and that the major achievements actually stemmed from it. (West in Drake 1973 p 59)
> . . . Discussions merely of things the railroad did are of no use unless we know whether these services represent more or less than would have been contributed by alternative investments. (Fogel in Drake 1973 pp 121–2)
> . . . Moreover, with one out of every four of the bushels [of wheat] produced in these states [ie Ohio, Michigan, Indiana and Illinois] sold in the East and South, it is clear that commercial agriculture was well under way in the Old Northwest long before the era of substantial railroad construction. (Fogel in Drake 1973 p 123)
> . . . [Fogel demonstrates that '76 per cent of all agricultural land by value' could have been exploited without the railway]. This finding does not support the frequently met contention that railroads were essential to the commercial exploitation of the prairies. (Fogel in Drake 1973 p 127)

Answer SAQ 4 I would not accept any of these statements as they stand. My ranking, from most credible to least, would be b, c, a – though c and a could easily be transposed.

a Did you notice the implicit quantification throughout this extract, embodied in the words *most, part, hardly, something, many, more or less, for weeks together*? Also the trouble with this kind of statement is that it is based upon impressions gathered, one assumes, haphazardly and likely, therefore, to confirm one's initial views. A statement like 'we have met with families . . .' could have described the experience of anyone who cared to meet families even in the 'most instructed and virtuous' part of the kingdom. The statement in fact tells us very little.

b   I regard this statement as the most credible one because it was based upon a quantitative assessment of the situation. In an ideal world one would wish to check it out; in particular to see what 'more extensive' meant and to examine the nature of the survey carried out by the Statistical Society. If one couldn't do this one could still be reassured by the fact that if Kay's statement had been an inaccurate reading of the report, it could have been challenged. Knowing this Kay would be likely to exercise care before making the statement. By contrast the statement in the quotation from the *Edinburgh Review* above could not be checked and, therefore, one's confidence in it must be small.

c   There are several features of this statement worth noting in the context of this unit. Firstly, it is used here to support the statement that 'there is no evidence to suggest that before 1833 the number of children employees of eight years and under was large'. The statement refers, however, to the year *1838*, five years *after* the first 'effectively policed' Factory Act forbade the employment of children of eight years and under. A second point to note lies in the wording of the statement; '37 out of 2,466 children under ten years (ie $1\frac{1}{2}$ per cent) *were found at work*' (my italics). Does this mean they were literally 'found at work', in the sense of being seen and counted? Or does it mean that this number of children were *reported* to be at work – by parents, perhaps, who may or may not have been evading the provisions of the act? Thirdly, given a situation where there was little readily available proof of birth dates (civil registration of births began only in 1837 and was not comparable, in efficiency, with present-day standards until the 1860s), it was easy to lie about one's age – if, in fact, one knew what that age was. I remember once coming across an abnormally large number of men in the Norwegian Census of 1801 whose age was given as thirty-six years. Not until I discovered that thirty-six years put one just outside the age of conscription was the puzzle solved!

Answer SAQ 5

1	**Topic of interest**	– Population change.
2	**Articulate problem**	– Are 'demographic principles' transcultural?
3	**Formulate hypothesis**	– Mortality is the major determinant of population change in pre-industrial societies.
4	**Devise test**	– Examine fertility, nuptiality and mortality in pre-industrial societies: historically in the West, currently in the rest of the world.
5	**Collect data**	– Parish registers of baptisms and burials; censuses; hearth counts; contemporary opinions; diets; medical reports; nutritional studies.
6	**Test**	– Devise measures of fertility, nuptiality and mortality appropriate for the available data (eg crude rates; vital index; proportions married; child:woman ratios; age-weighted marital fertility rate).
7	**Result**	– Hypothesis that mortality is the major determinant of population change in pre-industrial societies not confirmed.

3

VI. State for each principal Teacher separately :—

	In Boys' or Mixed Department under Master	In Girls' or Mixed Department under Mistress.	In Infants' Department	In Evening, if not Employed in School at other Meetings.
	+285 3.391 2.111	26.58 29.49		
1. Name.	Henry Smith	Sophia Ann Smith	Fanny Luck.	
Exact date of Birth.	May 14. 1834	Nov 4 1852	25 March 1860.	
Exact date of entrance upon duty in this School.	Appointed Nov 13 1879 but duties will not Commence till after Xmas holidays	Appointed Nov 13. 1879 but duties will not Commence till after Xmas holidays.	Appointed 13 Nov 1879 but duties will not Commence after Xmas Holidays.	
How long a Teacher of Elementary Schools?	25 years	8 years	5 years Pupil teacher and 1 year Assistant Mistress.	
Do the Managers certify to good Character and Conduct?	Yes	Yes	Yes.	
2. Whether Certificated	Yes	Yes	Provisionally Certificated.	
a. Date.	1853	1874 (3rd Class) 2nd Class (1878)	30 September 1878.	
b. Class.	First Class			
If not yet Certificated, state, if annual grants are applied for,— (1.) Whether willing to be examined. (2.) Whether a Candidate for a Certificate under article 59.				
3. Whether formerly apprenticed as a Pupil Teacher, and if so, in what School?	Yes. Winchester Central	No	Yes A. Chester Mission School Northampton.	
4. Whether trained—		No	No	
a. Name of Training School.	Yes Winchester	—		
b. Date of Entry.	Sept 1852			
c. Date of Quitting.	March 1854			
d. Whether examined for a Certificate?	Yes	Yes		
5. Whether formerly engaged in a School under Inspection, and if so,—	Yes	Yes	Yes. St Judes Southwark October 1878 to 25 July 1879 Girls British School Folkstone. 28 July 1879 to 7 November 1879—	
a. In what School?	Potton Board	Potton Board		
b. Date of Entry.	June 1876 not yet left (left at Xmas)	June 1876 not yet left (left at Xmas).		
c. Date of Quitting.				
6. How many Scholars (upon an average) have attended the department of each Principal Teacher during the last six months? See note (a) in p. 2, § IV	50 (at Heyford)	60.— (at Heyford)	There has not been any provision made for Infants.	

Note. the Teachers Engagements date from 25 December 1879; and owing to the Christmas Holidays the actual work of the School Commenced 5 January 1880.

Contents   Unit 2

Objectives

After studying this unit you should be able to:

1 Give *two* advantages of sampling for students of Applied Historical Studies.

2 Obtain a sample using a table of random numbers.

3 Describe the method of taking a systematic sample and its possible shortcomings.

4 Define the following:
statistical population; sampling bias; sampling error; sampling frame; random sample; systematic sample; mean; parameter; statistic; histogram; bar chart; normal curve.

*5 List ways in which sampling bias may affect judgments based on samples and methods of avoiding such bias.

* Embraces objectives for first radio programme, *Sampling Historical Data*.

Sampling

1 Why sample?

. . . There was once a man who did not believe in sampling, and who campaigned against it up and down the country. He emphasized all the dangers . . . pointing out in particular that sampling was necessarily based on probabilities rather than on certainties, so that you could never really be *sure* that your conclusions were correct. One day he was due to give a lecture on the evils of sampling in a nearby town. He got up, and went down to breakfast. His egg did not look too good, so he tasted a bit of it, found that it seemed all right, and finished the lot. He put his hand outside the door, felt that it was raining, and decided to take an umbrella. He looked in the rack for a magazine to read in the train, thumbed through one or two, found one that looked interesting, and put it in his pocket. When the train pulled into the station he chose the carriage that looked the cleanest and travelled to the nearby town. He went to the lecture hall, and gave his anti-sampling lecture, which was received with rapturous applause by an audience of about a hundred people. 'How did it go?', his wife asked him when he got home again. 'Wonderful, wonderful', the man replied, 'it's obvious that there's a very strong feeling in the country against sampling.' (Meek 1971 p 72)

A moment's reflection should be enough to convince anyone that sampling is an every-day occurrence. We all observe other people sampling; all of us take samples and we are all subject to the sampling exercises of others. For instance I remember, as a boy (I have got to that terrible stage where boyhood memories flood back more readily than those of yesterday!), watching my mother sampling the temperature of her oven by sticking her elbow into it. I also remember her sampling the inside of a cake by sticking a needle into it, when she took it out of the oven. If the needle emerged as clean as it went in, the cake was apparently 'done': if it had mixture sticking to its sides, it was not, so back in the oven it went.

So far as you and this course are concerned, I shall be sampling your knowledge of its content, and your skills in applying that knowledge, by asking you to do tutor-marked and computer-marked assignments and, at the end of the year, a three-hour examination. When I switch on my television to watch a play, or a football match, what I see is in part the result of a sampling exercise carried out by some theatrical producer or team selector. Both will probably have chosen the participants in their respective 'shows' on the basis of some direct, or indirect, sampling of their footballing skills or acting abilities.

Sometimes our attempts at sampling are frustrated: who has not seen the sign on the display of tomatoes in a vegetable market – 'Don't squeeze me till I'm yours'. And sometimes the sampling exercise itself has become a ritual, its original manifest function long since abandoned. How many people, for instance, tell those imperious waiters to put their wine, after that first sip, anywhere but into their customers' glasses?

Now in all the cases I have mentioned, sampling is carried out because we do not have the time, the energy, the patience, the money or the opportunity of doing anything else. We sample because we want to generalize about the temperature of the oven, the state of the cake, the student's success in following the course, the footballer's skill, the actor's ability, the quality of the tomatoes we want to buy or the wine we want to drink. In each case, it is a knowledge of the *whole*, whatever it is, we are after, when for a variety of reasons we can only have access to a *part* of it.

Why sampling is so important for this course is that we too want to generalize, or to put it more formally, we want to be able to make *general statements* about different kinds of phenomena. And we are dealing with large amounts of data – baptisms, burials, marriages, votes, schools, teachers, households, migrants etc. So it may only be possible to have direct experience of a small part of the material. The problem is how to draw our sample. Can we adopt the rule of thumb methods

Page 27.

BAPTISMS solemnized in the Parish of *Wendover*
in the County of *Bucks* in the Year 18/7

When Baptized.	Child's Christian Name.	Parents Name.		Abode.	Quality, Trade, or Profession.	By whom the Ceremony was performed.
		Christian.	Surname.			
1817. Sept.ʳ 21ˢᵗ No. 209.	Thomas Son of	Joseph & Ann	Langstone	Wendover	Labourer	C Turnor Vicar
21ˢᵗ No. 210.	Elizabeth Daur. of	William & Charlotte	Croxford	Wendover	Farmer	C Turnor Vicar
Octr. 5ᵗʰ No. 211.	Charles Son of	William & Mary	Frantham	Wendover	Farmer	C Turnor Vicar
26ᵗʰ No. 212.	Jane Daur. of	Richard & Julia	Holland	Wendover	Bricklayer	C Turnor Vicar
26ᵗʰ No. 213.	Sarah Daur. of	Joseph & Lydia	Dancer	Wendover	Labourer	C Turnor Vicar
Novr. 9ᵗʰ No. 214.	William Son of	John & Mary	Wells	Wendover	Labourer	C Turnor Vicar
30ᵗʰ No. 215.	John Son of	William & Mary	Payne	Wendover	Labourer	C Turnor Vicar
30ᵗʰ No. 216.	Elizabeth Daur. of	William & Fabie	Jennings	Wendover	Labourer	C Turnor Vicar

described earlier in this unit? Can we, like my mother with her oven, just dip into the material, or as with the tomatoes, can we squeeze out sufficient information from a small part of the available data to enable us to assess the whole? As it happens, social scientists often do just this (see Erikson in Drake 1973 pp 17–18). For example, a Yale psychologist, Kenneth Kenniston, wrote a book entitled *Young Radicals*. In this he drew general conclusions about student radicalism. The basis for these conclusions was a number of interviews with *fourteen students*, eleven men and three women. Works of this kind are usually described by their authors as 'case studies' which as Thernstrom has pointed out (in Swierenga 1970 p 72) 'lends an attractive aura of generality' to one's research. But does it in fact do so? Is it anything more than a confidence trick?

> . . . Historians and sociologists alike have been reluctant to consider such questions. Thus William F. Whyte's classic field report on youth in the North End [of Boston, Massachusetts], *Streetcorner Society*, leaves us in the dark as to how much of what the author describes reflects basic patterns of working class life in American cities, and how much is due to the particular ethnic group (Italians), the particular neighbourhood (the North End), or the particular historical period (the late 30s) Whyte dealt with. Nor does Herbert Gans' interesting recent work, *The Urban Villagers*, which treats working class Italo-Americans in the West End in the late 50s, go very far beyond *Streetcorner Society* in this respect. (Swierenga 1970 p 72)

One might even argue that these particular studies, and others like them, are much less satisfactory than my mother's elbow in giving us information from which to generalize. The reason is that in all research one is moving into the unknown: one's task is 'to boldly go where no man has gone before' (*Star Trek*, BBC 1, Friday nights 1973). Of course one goes into research armed with a battery of techniques and a wealth of experience, accumulated directly or vicariously. Nevertheless, one is attempting, in the sort of endeavour we are engaged upon in this course, to explore new materials, or old materials in new ways. And because of this unless we are very careful, our sample may be a very *biased* one. My mother's cakes turned out fine because the technique she used to find out the temperature of the oven or the consistency of the cake on any particular occasion were backed by years of experience; or, to put it another way, on hundreds of samples. Over the years she must have put her elbow into many different parts of *her* oven; her needle must have gone into many different parts of the cake. And in buying tomatoes she knew that some shopkeepers bought only graded supplies, so that one tomato was very much like another in size, colour, ripeness, taste and so on. But with other, unknown suppliers, no matter how many notices and frowns from the shopkeeper she received, she would only select those tomatoes she *had* pinched and passed as satisfactory. In other words she would not sample.

So far we have made three points. First, that sampling is very much a part of our day-to-day lives. Second, we sample because we want to know something about the whole *population* of which the sample is, by definition, only a part and we are unable to explore every part of that population. Thirdly, we must be careful how we draw the sample, especially if we are exploring new territory, otherwise the sample will not represent the population. It will be a biased sample. This last point has important implications for our use of sampling which we shall now proceed to explore.

2 How to draw a sample

The first essential in sampling is to ensure that the sample represents, as nearly as possible, the population from which it is drawn. To bring this about is rarely easy and quite often is very difficult indeed. It is, however, an essential first stage and no amount of statistical wizardry in the analysis of results can compensate for a badly drawn, and therefore probably biased, sample. The skills required for this process are

'Population' is *not* used here in the everyday sense of a number of people living in a particular area. In statistics, the concept of population refers not to people but to observations. A set of people can, therefore, be a *statistical population*, but so can a collection of tomatoes, a stack of magazines, a line of railway carriages, a collection of Intelligence Quotients and so on.

not especially quantitative: far more important is the ability to examine a situation 'in the round' (a traditional historian's skill), so that no features likely to affect the population, and hence the sample, are ignored. In order to examine the problems involved in drawing samples, we will look at them in the context of an actual example. Let us take McClelland's piece in the course reader (Drake 1973 pp 31-51).

The first part of this chapter is based on an article by Bradburn and Berlew (1961). In this the two scholars report their findings from an experiment in which they sought to demonstrate a particular relationship between *n* Achievement and economic growth in England. As they detail their hypothesis in a commendably explicit manner I cite it here:

> ... The specific hypothesis to be tested in this study may be formulated in its strongest terms as follows: an increase in *n* Achievement level in England from time period A to time period B will result in economic growth from time period B to time period C; and similarly, a decrease in *n* Achievement level from A to B will result in economic decline from B to C, when time periods A, B and C represent 50-year periods in English history.
> (Bradburn and Berlew 1961 p 10)

In order to test the hypothesis they drew a sample from English literature. What lay behind this was their belief that just as one could measure *n* Achievement in the individual 'by systematically investigating the types of images he uses and the ways in which he represents situations', so at the 'societal level' one could measure *n* Achievement by 'applying an adaptation of the scoring scheme used with individuals to the imaginative literature of a society' (Bradburn and Berlew 1961 p 9). They, therefore, searched their sample of literature for phrases (given here in italics) like the following (Bradburn and Berlew 1961 p 11):

> ... as they may *excel in knowledge* of liberal sciences, for if we being unlearned have by industrye heaped up sufficient store ... then may they *by learning aspire unto greater promotion*, and *builde greater matters upon a better foundation*.
> (George Gascoigne, *The Glasse of Government*, 1575, drama)

> In days of yore, where statesmen wore
> Clean hands and honest faces,
> No feuds were then among great men, nor striving for high places.
> *Their only aim was lasting fame.*
> *Their virtues made them great, Sir.*
> (*Wilkin's Political Ballads*, Vol II c 1740)

In drawing up their sample Bradburn and Berlew sought ways to minimize the possibility of bias. Some of these are detailed in the course reader (Drake 1973 pp 32-4) and will not be repeated here. Others are given in their article. First they sought to make as complete a list of authors as possible. Put in the language of sampling, they sought to create as complete a *sampling frame* as possible. Sometimes the sampling frame is ready to hand. For instance, for the exercises in sampling I shall be inviting you to do, I am sending out with the course material for this block a reprint of the *Bath Poll Book* for the parliamentary by-election held in that city in 1855. Here the sampling frame is provided by the list of votes cast for the two candidates. Our sample will then be a sum that is drawn in some way from this total number of votes and will, by definition, be less than that number. In this case creating a sampling frame was easy, certainly when compared with the work Bradburn and Berlew had to do. Once they had their sampling frame, the two scholars drew a *random* sample from it so as to 'eliminate any bias resulting from the literary preferences of the person choosing the sample' (Bradburn and Berlew 1961 p 10).

This element of randomness is crucial to all scientific sampling, by which I mean all sampling which purports to represent, as accurately as possible, the population from which the sample is drawn. It is easy to grasp this once one thinks of the many examples of non-random sampling which surround us in our everyday lives. For

Figure 2 Page from 1851 census enumerator's book, Ashford, Kent

Parish or Township of Ashford	Ecclesiastical District of	Town of Ashford							
No. of Schedule	Name of Street, Place, or Road, and Name or No. of House	Name and Surname of each Person who abode in the house, on the Night of the 30th March, 1851	Relation to Head of Family	Condition	Age of Males	Age of Females	Rank, Profession, or Occupation	Where Born	Whether Blind, or Deaf-and-Dumb
64	High St	Wm Huston	Head	Mar	53		Cwil & stationary Engineer	Kent Ashford	
		Mary Ann do	Dawr	M		18	Athome	do	
		Francis C do	Son	U	16		Scholar	do	
		Edward W do	Son				do	do	
		Charles H do	Son				do	do	
		Laura Bearyan	Visitor	U				Mid Romney	
		Sarah Hanes	Serut	U	23		Doctor Solicitor	Hythlis	
		Elizabeth Beal	do	U	22		Cooks Housekeeper	Hythlis	
					23		House Serv	Smarder	
65	High St	James Hicks	do	U	84		Groom Serv	Brighton Mx	
		Elizabeth Dutnee	Head				Landholder	Ashford	
		John St do	Son	U	49		Retired Merchant	Surry Creht	
		Michael Do	Dawr	U	42		Found children	do do	
		Margaret Boyd	Serv	U	32		Found children	Wales Bristol	
		Mary Bourne	do	U	21		House Serv	Kent Wrockshar	
66	High St	Henry Whitfeld	Head	U	44		do	Ashford	
		William do	Brothe	U			MHestr SSDeneral Accountant	do	
		Edwin do	do	U			BA Cambridge	do	
		John Mason	Medical Asst	U			Medical Asist	Warwick Warmington	
		Ft Fitzgerald	House Pupil	U			Article Clerk	Kent Newnham	
		Samuel Warrington	Serv	U			Groom	Brock	
							Total of Persons....	11	

example, to return to our earlier illustrations, our friendly neighbourhood green-grocer sometimes decorates his display of oranges with a half dozen or so which he has cut in two, so we can see the juicy flesh. We know of course that if, when carrying out this process, he had cut open a dehydrated one, it would have disappeared promptly into his waste bin. Again, theatre managers are adept at giving us a sample of reviews – or more precisely, extracts of reviews – of the shows they are presenting. They are, of course, uniformly good! Or to take a final example, if our anti-sampling lecturer, whom we introduced at the beginning of this unit, instead of choosing something to read from his own magazine rack, had gone to the station bookshop and cast his eye along the paperback covers, he would have been offered, by the publishers, a visual sample of their literary content. As many of us have found out such samples are non-random in the extreme!

In all the cases above we are implying that some deliberate distortion has taken place. Frequently, however, even when every attempt is made to avoid bias, it nevertheless creeps in. In fact, there is only one way to produce a truly random sample and that is to leave the process of selection entirely to chance. We can do this by using a table of random numbers. One of these appears in the Appendix below. These tables are produced in such a way that at any point in the table any number or

Figure 3 Page from *The Bath Poll Book*, **1855**

LIST OF PERSONS

WHO

VOTED FOR W. WHATELEY, ESQ.

RATING.

A

Abbott William, 4, Burlington street, gentleman	£45
Abraham George, 25, New King street, gentleman	28
Acton Edward H., 4, Great Bedford street, clergyman	55
Adams George, 5, St. James's street, confectioner	60
Alexander Robert, Lyncombe vale, florist	30
Alexander William, 15, New Bond street, shirt maker	75
Allen John, 5, Lambridge buildings, builder	18
Anderdon William Proctor, 14, St. James's sq., captain	110
Andrews Frederick, Winifred lane, gardener	20
Angell William, 19, Catherine place, tailor	60
Anstey John Thos., 18, Lansdown crescent, gentleman	100
Antell Robert, 44, St. James's sq., lodging house keeper	70
Anthony David, 3, Hanover street and 8, Ladymead, pawnbroker	47
Archer Charles, 4, Southcot place, sexton	18
Armstrong James, near Henrietta bdgs., cabinet maker	11
Arnold Henry, Upland villa, gentleman	16
Arnold Robert Brooks, 2, Stall street, wine merchant	75
Arter Isaac, 13, Bladud buildings, gentleman	60
Ashfield Arthur, 28, Circus, gentleman	140
Ashley James, 12, Axford buildings, gentleman	40
Ashman Charles, 13, Green street, baker	50
Ashman Frederick, 29, New King street, lodging house keeper	28
Ashplant John, 7, St. Andrew's terrace, livery stable keeper	45
Ashton Thomas, 3, Burlington street, draper's assistant	43
Asprey Francis, 16, Southgate street, grocer	55
Atkins William Henry, 16, Kensington pl., gentleman	65
Austin James, 1, Larkhall place, gentleman	22
Austin John, 20, Pulteney street, general	90
Awdry Jeremiah, 14, Johnstone street, clergyman	50
Aylmer Thomas Brabazon, 3, Cambridge pl., gentleman	60

B

Bagshawe Edward Benjamin, 1, Cavendish crescent, clergyman	70

3

Figure 4 Computer printout showing entries from 1851 and 1861 census
enumerators' books of Ashford, Kent, sorted and merged by the computer into
alphabetical order. See Figure 2 for some of original source.

H	0	613	0	1	2	2THURSBY	JANE		27Y	2	8HYTHE	KENT	1HOUSEKEEPR	8	0	0
H	0	613	0	1	1	1THURSBY	JOHN		39Y	1	1HYTHE	KENT	1SHOEMAKERJ	1	0	0
H	0	613	0	1	3	3THURSBY	JOHN		3Y	1	13ASHFORD	KENT	1	13	0	0
H	0	457	0	1	1	1THURSBY	WILLIAM		36Y	1	1HYTHE	KENT	1TANNER	1	0	0
H	2	327	0	1	1	1THURSBY	WILLIAM		44Y	1	1HYTHE	KENT	2LABOURER	1	0	0
H	0	820	14	1	1	1THURSTON	ANN		53Y	2	1ASHFORD	KENT	2CIVILENGWF	1	0	0
H	2	246	14	1	2	2THURSTON	ANNE		63Y	2	2ASHFORD	KENT	2	2	0	0
H	0	820	14	1	5	5THURSTON	CHARLES	H	6Y	1	3ASHFORD	KENT	1SCHOLAR	3	0	0
H	2	246	14	1	6	6THURSTON	CHARLES	H	16Y	1	3ASHFORD	KENT	1ENGINCLERK	3	0	0
H	0	820	14	1	4	4THURSTON	EDWARD	W	9Y	1	3ASHFORD	KENT	1SCHOLAR	3	0	0
H	2	246	14	1	5	5THURSTON	EDWARD	W	19Y	1	3ASHFORD	KENT	1MEDICSTUDE	3	0	0
H	0	820	14	1	3	3THURSTON	FRANCIS		15Y	1	3ASHFORD	KENT	1SCHOLAR	3	0	0
H	0	802	52	1	7	7THURSTON	JOHN		19Y	1	17ASHFORD	KENT	1PAINTER	17	0	0
H	2	246	14	1	4	4THURSTON	LOUISA		23Y	2	4ASHFORD	KENT	1	4	0	0
H	0	820	14	1	2	2THURSTON	MARY	A	19Y	2	4ASHFORD	KENT	1	4	0	0
H	2	246	14	1	3	3THURSTON	MARY	A	28Y	2	4ASHFORD	KENT	1	4	0	0
H	2	246	14	1	1	1THURSTON	THOMAS		62Y	1	1WILLESBOROKENT		2CIVILENGNR	1	0	0
H	2	894	0	1	4	4TICKNER	ALBERT		6Y	1	17ASHFORD	KENT	1	17	0	0
H	2	1303	0	1	3	3TICKNER	CLARA		1Y	2	4ASHFORD	KENT	1	4	0	0
H	2	1303	0	1	1	1TICKNER	GEORGE		27Y	1	1LYMPNE	KENT	2LABOURER	1	0	0

sequence of numbers has an equal chance of appearing next. To use such a table is easy, though laborious, if that is not too much of a paradox. Let's take an example.

Turn to the copy of the *Bath Poll Book* for 1855. Suppose we want to draw a random sample of Whateley's votes. We are told he got 1,129 votes (see p 24) so our sampling frame is provided by that number. Unfortunately, our voters are not numbered, so our first task is to assign a number to each. Already the mind boggles! However, to reduce this job a bit it is only necessary to label every tenth name, ie William Abbott will be number one; John Thos Anstey number eleven; Charles Ashman, number twenty-one and so on. When we have done this we find that only 1,126 votes are recorded in the poll book, not 1,129 as given in the summary, which is a salutary reminder to check our data whenever this is possible.

We are now in a position to draw our random sample. Let us suppose we want a sample of fifty names. We turn to our table of random sampling numbers. We find the numbers are grouped in fours and each four is divided in half. Now if our sampling frame embraced under 100 voters we could choose our sample either by going down one of these columns of pairs until we had got our fifty, or by going horizontally across the page. For instance, if we started in the top left-hand corner of page 61 and worked downwards, we would choose the voters numbered 20, 74, 94, 22, 93, 45 and so on, ie James Ashley; Henry Bethell; Edmund Boult; Frederick Ashman; James Boord; John Luce Barfoot etc. But we could have begun in the same place with twenty and gone horizontally to 17, 42, 28, 23 and so on, ie James Ashley; Robert Brooks Arnold; Thomas Baldwin; John Austin; John Ashplant etc. Alternatively, we could have started at the top of the third column from the left and gone down which would have given us voters 42, 4, 49, 78, 12, 77 etc; or begun at the sixth number down in column seven from the top left and proceeded horizontally. We should then have had voters 99, 45, 52, 95, 69 etc.

We have, in reality, a rather different situation. For we have 1,126 voters which means we have to choose from numbers of up to four figures, ie from 1 to 9,999. This is a little unfortunate from our point of view because it means that many numbers in the table are greater than 1,126 and therefore cannot be used by us. Let us suppose we start at the twenty-first number down the first column on the left of our table. This number is 872. As this is less than 1,126 we can draw it. So our first entry in the sample is James Shutter. The next number, however, is 9,597 which is no use to us; nor is the next, 3,799. The one after that, 579, is all right and adds John Lane to our sample. But we then have to reject twenty more numbers before coming to 723, which gives us our third contribution to the sample in the

Figure 5 Record of a naval officer's career. Source: Public Record Office, ADM 196/42

468

NAME— *Raymond Abelard Langley Azzard*

Date of Birth ... 30 *[baptized]* Parish
... *April 1867* ... Place of Birth ... *Hawksden Park, Sussex*

Name and Profession of Father ... } *J. W. Azzard on*
Knights Park, Chipstone Kingsbridge } Date and Place of Marriage ...

Dates of Orders and Commissions.	Rewards and Distinctions.	Examinations.	Special Attainments or Qualifications.
4 June 1883 Midshipman 14 June 1889 Acting Lieut. in Sept. 1889 Lieutenant 1 April 1891 Lieutenant	*Married. 1 month's leave on proof out of Britannia.* *Egyptian Medal 1883.*	*Passed for Mid. 3rd Cl. Cert.: 610 marks* *Passed Instructorship for Seaman Midshipmen by* *Board Examiners July 24 aug 89 3rd Cl. Cert: 610 marks* *Failed to pass College March 1888.* *Passed College June 88 3rd Cl. Cert: 831 marks* *— Torpedo Septbr 88 2nd Cl. Cert: 160 marks* *— Gunnery Jan 89 2nd Cl. Cert: 463 marks* *— Pilotage March 89 3rd Cl. Cert: 727 marks*	

SHIP.	Station.	Date of Appointment.	Date of Discharge.	Cause.	Date of Report.	General Conduct.	Ability.	Zeal.	Judgment.	Temper.	Professional Knowledge.	If Temperate.	Physical Qualities.	Performance of Special Duties.	If deserving of advancement.	REMARKS.
Britannia	*Training Ship*	*15 July 80*	*29 July 82*		*July 82*	*G.*	*Poor*				*F.*	*Yes*				*Captain Mill*
Achille	*Medtn.*	*8 Aug 82*	*1 Nov 82*		*Apr 83*	*V.9.*	*F.*				*F.*	*Yes*	*very steady but zealous*			*— " Fane*
Northampton	*N Am*	*1 Nov 82*	*13 Oct 82*		*Jan 85*	*V.G*	*F.*				*G.*	*Yes*	*[attentive to duties? nothing]*			*— " Cleveland*
Tudor	*"*	*14 Oct 82*	*7 Nov 88*		*Sept 85*	*V.G.*	*V.G*				*G.*	*Yes*	*very good health*			*— " Clayton*
Alexandra dll Ms	*"*	*23 Nov 83*	*21 Dec 85*	*Arrival on Royal Yacht [?]*	*5 Nov 87*	*V.G.*	*V.G*				*G.*	*Yes*				*— " "*
Superb	*"*	*22 Dec 85*	*30 Apr [?]*	*transferred Superb*	*[?]*	*V.G.*	*G.*				*v.G.*	*Yes*	*Has shown much zeal on [?]*			*Captain Osborne. Floyd*
Diamond	*[?]*	*11 Oct 84*	*June 89*	*by [?]*	*[?]*	*V.G.*	*G.*				*V.G*	*Yes*	*Much zeal and attention*			
[excellent?] [?]	*[?]*	*7 Sept 89*	*14 July 89*		*[?]*	*V.G*	*G.*				*G.*	*Yes*	*willing and painstaking*			*Capt Gray*

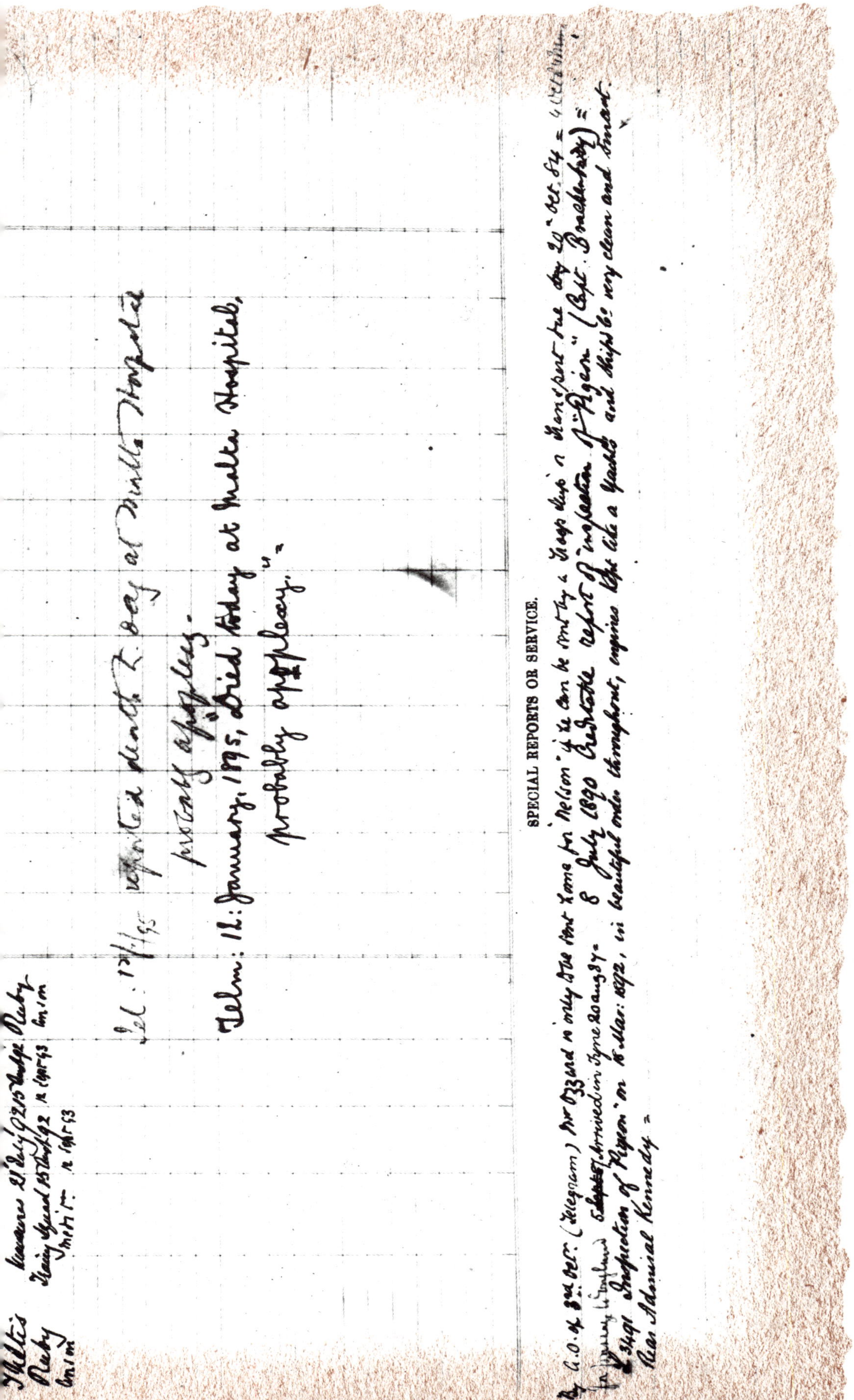

SPECIAL REPORTS OR SERVICE.

Vel. 17th/1/95 on deck 2. day at Malta Hospital
probably epileptic.

Telm: 12: January, 1895, Died today at Malta Hospital,
probably apoplexy."

[handwritten entries, largely illegible]

Ret. 3rd Dec. (Telegram) ... "Nelson" ... can be ... a long days ... transport ... day 24th Oct 84 ...
... arrived June 20 aug 84 ... 8 July 1890 Brisbane ... inspection ... "Pigin" ... (Capt. Brooksbury) ...
3491 Inspection of "Pigin" on 16 Mar: 1892 ... beautiful order throughout; inspires the life a yacht and ships 6: very clean and smart.
Rer. Admiral Kennedy."

shape of Matthew Parker. Now it is obvious that our task of selecting our sample by this method is being made more tedious by the fact that we have to reject so many numbers. We can, however, take a short cut. As Gregory (1971 p 102) tells us, we can (to take our total of 1,126) 'rephrase the numbers above 2,000 as repeats of the 1 to 2,000 series', so the numbers 2,000–3,999, 4,000–5,999, 6,000–7,999 etc can each be taken as repeats of our first 2,000. By adopting this method our rejection rate is very considerably reduced. To demonstrate this let us retrace the exercise we have just been carrying out.

We begin, as before, with the twenty-first number down the first column on the left of our table on p 61. This number is 872. We can use it. The next number is 9,597. This falls in the range 8,000–9,999 (ie the fifth of our groups of 2,000) and so we can renumber it 1,597. This is above 1,126 so we must discard it. The next number 3,799 falls in the 2,000–3,999 range (ie the second group of 2,000) and gives us 1,799. This is still above 1,126 and must, therefore, also be discarded. The next number is 579 and can be used quite straightforwardly. The next is 5,585. It falls in the 4,000–5,999 range (the third group of 2,000) and gives us 1,585. Again this is above 1,126 and must be discarded. So far our 'short-cut' is not proving very successful! But now our luck turns. The next three numbers – all of which had to be discarded using our 'long method' – can each be used. The number 6,728 falls into the 6,000–7,999 range (the fourth group of 2,000) and gives us 728. Then, 8,586 falls in the fifth group (ie 8,000–9,999) and gives us 586. Finally, 4,010 gives us 10, falling, as it does, in the third group of 2,000 which is 4,000–5,999.

It must by now be apparent that taking a random sample, though demanding no more than the ability to count and, using our short-cut method, to subtract, is nevertheless a time-consuming process. It is, however, conceptually the simplest method of sampling and in many practical situations the best method. It should be adopted wherever time, patience and the nature of the material itself permit. Why this is so is readily apparent when we turn to the technique of systematic sampling, another main method.

Systematic sampling involves taking every fifth, sixth, tenth, twentieth or whatever number we need to give us a sample of the size we want. For instance, if we wanted to draw a systematic sample of fifty votes from Whateley's votes in the *Bath Poll Book* we could take every twenty-second name. In this way, we would cover the whole population and end up with about fifty names (1,126 ÷ 22 = 51 and a bit over). As the calculation shows we would get fifty-one names but we could discard the final one, or, say, begin at number twenty-two (Frederick Ashman). Our next name would be William Ford Bally, our next James Beard and so on. This method is quite obviously much less time-consuming than is random sampling and in the case of the Bath voters is probably as good. The reason for this is that since the voters are listed alphabetically we have no cause to believe that our choice of every twenty-second name is likely to include more of one type of voter than of another: no cause to believe, in other words, that our sample would be biased. But often lists are biased in one way or another. Here is one example:

. . . During World War II, there was a research agency connected with the Army which was engaged in finding out how the soldiers felt on particular subjects. When a member of this organization went into a camp, he obtained a list of soldiers in the camp from which to draw a sample. An obviously convenient procedure was to draw a systematic sample from this list. In one particular instance in which such a sample was being drawn, some of the characteristics of those men drawn into the sample were examined. It was found that much too great a proportion of master sergeants were selected for the sample. Upon learning this, the surveyor had no trouble in finding the reason. The men in the camp were listed barracks by barracks. Within each barracks the men were listed in order of their military rank. Also there were the same number of men in each barracks. Unfortunately, the chosen sampling interval was such that it stepped off the same line-

Figure 6 Record of a soldier's career 1828–37. Source: Public Record Office, WO69/153/552.

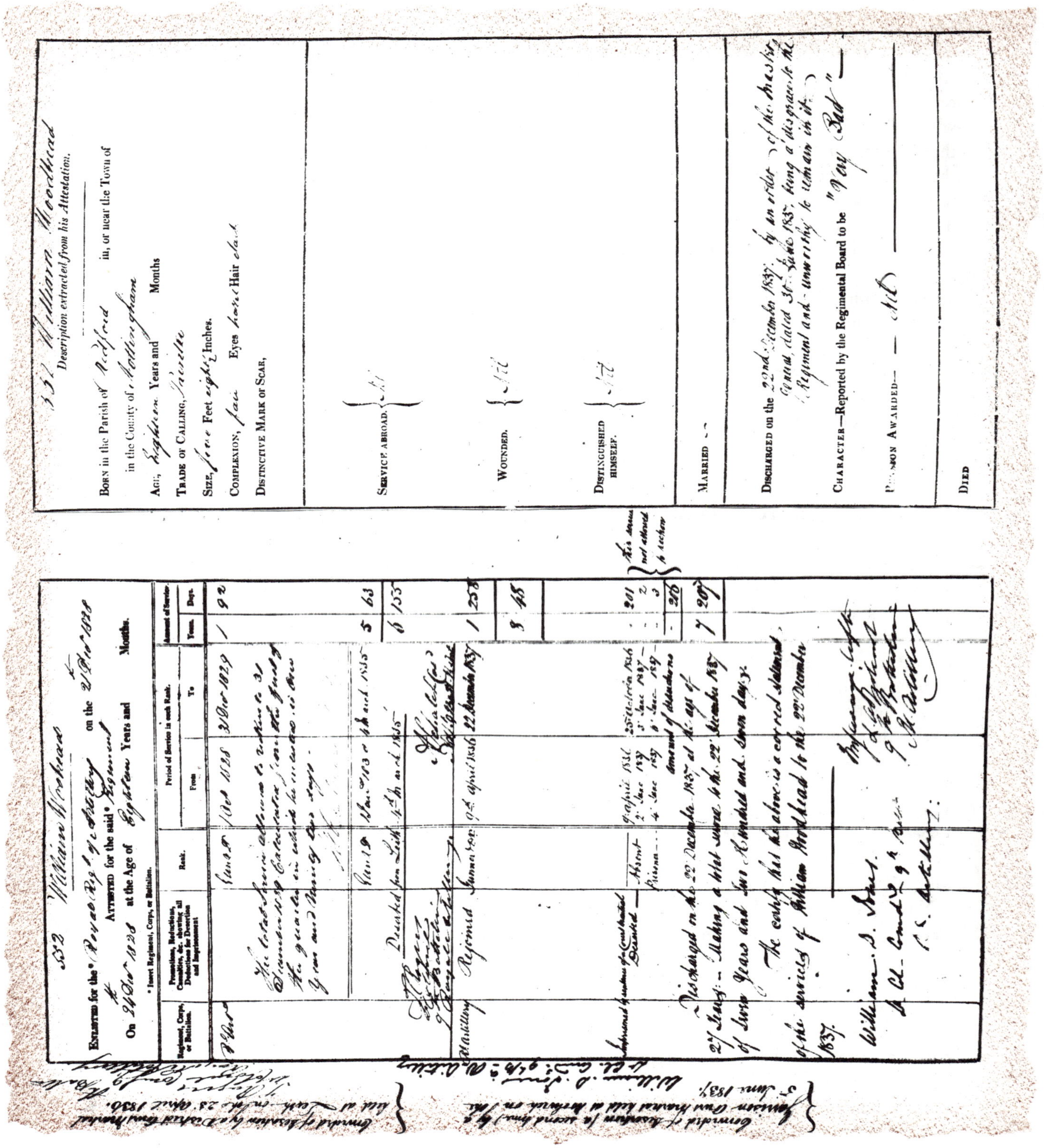

532 William Woodhead
Description extracted from his Attestation.

Born in the Parish of Radford in, or near the Town of
in the County of Nottingham
Age, Eighteen Years and Months
Trade or Calling, Presser
Size, Five Feet eight½ Inches.
Complexion, fair Eyes hazel Hair dark
Distinctive Mark or Scar,

Service Abroad. Nil
Wounded. Nil
Distinguished himself. Nil

Married —

Discharged on the 22nd December 1837, by an order of the Master General dated 30th June 1837, being a disgrace to the Regiment and unworthy to remain in it.

Character.—Reported by the Regimental Board to be "Very Bad" —

Pension Awarded — Nil —

Died

532 William Woodhead

Enlisted for the Royal Regt of Artillery on the 21st Oct 1828
Attested for the said Regiment
On 24 Oct 1828 at the Age of Eighteen Years and Months.

* Insert Regiment, Corps, or Battalion.

Regiment, Corps, or Battalion.	Promotions, Reductions, Casualties, &c. showing all Deductions for Desertion and Imprisonment	Rank.	Period of Service in each Rank. From	To	Amount of Service. Years.	Days.
R Artillery		Gunner	21 Oct 1828	21 Oct 1829	1	92
	The total service allowed to reckon is 31 December 1829 Calculated from the period he arrived in which he ... years and ... days					
		Gunner	... 1830	... 1835	5	63
	Deserted from Leith ... 1835				6	155
Artillery	Rejoined	Gunner	9 April 1836	22 December 1837	1	258
					8	48
	Imprisoned ... Court Martial ... Absent — Prison — Deducted		9 April 1836 / 2 June 1837 / 4 June 1837	25 October 1836 / 3 June 1837 / 6 June 1837	-	201 / 2 / 3
					-	206
					7	207

This service not allowed to reckon

Discharged on the 22 December 1837, at the age of 27 Years: — Making a total service to the 22 December 1837 of Seven Years and Two Hundred and Seven days.

The certify that the above is a correct statement of the services of William Woodhead to the 22nd December 1837.

William S. ... Lt. Col. Comdg 9th Battn R. Artillery

Convicted of Desertion by District Court Martial held at Leith on the 23 April 1836.

Convicted of Desertion (a second time) by a General Court Martial held at Woolwich on the 5th June 1837.

numbers on list after list, and in this way it happened to fall again and again on lines that usually contained the names of master sergeants. (Stephan and McCarthy 1963 p 33)

Let us now return to the sample of literature drawn by Bradburn and Berlew. We left them at the point where a random sample was being drawn 'to *eliminate any bias* resulting from the literary preferences of the person choosing the sample'. We return now in order to mention two of the other factors taken into account by them when producing their sampling frame. These were first that in choosing the literature they sought for the most imaginative. This was because they wanted to 'minimize the effects of current conditions and topical subjects', believing 'on the basis of psychological research that the more fanciful and "unreal" the material, the more motives . . . influence the content' (Bradburn and Berlew 1961 p 10). Second, they concentrated their attention on drama, street ballads and accounts of sea voyages, because they wanted to reduce the 'bias due to level of literacy'. Since drama and street ballads were 'performed' verbally they obviously served this purpose.

To sum up this section: we have tried to demonstrate how taking a sample involves a great deal of judgement. It is far more than a numerical exercise. Indeed that part of it is relatively straightforward and is more a test of patience than of intellect. We must now turn to the question of what our sample tells us and, equally, what it does not. Once we have done this we can return to several other aspects of drawing a sample.

3   How to interpret a sample

In order to simplify the exposition in this section we shall take as the population, about which we wish to know more, the votes cast in the Bath election of 1855. And in order to simplify the arithmetic we will begin by looking at just eight votes. These are the first eight votes listed for Tite. Let us imagine that these eight votes represent all the votes cast for Tite. They are the sampling frame. Let us further imagine that we are trying to estimate just one *parameter* of this population. A parameter is the name given to any numerical characteristic of a *population*. For example, the proportion of gentlemen among our population of voters is a parameter, ie it is $\frac{1}{8}$ or $1 \div 8$. Again, the *mean* rateable value of the premises occupied by our population of voters is £24$\frac{3}{8}$

ie £36 + £20 + £20 + £17 + £30 + £38 + £10 + £24 = £195 ÷ 8.

This too is a parameter. A numerical characteristic of a *sample* is called a statistic, a special use of the singular form of statistics. It is easy to remember the distinction by noting that the two words beginning with 'p' go together and the two beginning with 's': population – parameter and sample – statistic.

Now let us suppose that we want to know the mean rateable value of the property which enfranchised Tite's voters. Remember at this time the vote was only given to men who had property of a certain value. We could find this *precisely* by adding up the value given against the name of each of Tite's voters and then dividing this sum by the number of his voters. This is a daunting task even with only 1,176 voters and a total value of £39,227. Imagine what it would be like with 10,000 voters and some £400,000 rateable value. Obviously, if we can get some idea of the mean value by taking a sample we would be spared much effort. Well, we can take a sample, either a random one or a systematic one, in the ways described above. But how do we know that the sample will give us a statistic (the mean rateable value of the sample) that is reasonably close to the parameter (the mean rateable value of the voters in the whole population) we are seeking? There are obviously tens of thousands of *different* samples that could be drawn. How much confidence can we have in ours?

To get somewhere near an answer to these questions, let us return to the first eight of Tite's voters. These are for our purposes the population we are dealing with. The parameter we are seeking is the mean rateable value of the property held by

You may perhaps have realized that in trying to eliminate one form of bias, Bradburn and Berlew are introducing another. For example, in looking for 'imaginative literature' in order, partly, to 'minimize the effects of current conditions and topical subjects' they may be excluding areas of writing which could tell quite a lot about *n* Achievement. However, the point to note here is that the bias imported in this way is recognized. It is explicit and can, therefore, be allowed for. The bias they excluded would have remained implicit in the material, unless the crucially important search for bias, which must precede all sampling, had been carried out.

In everyday language when we speak of the 'average' we almost invariably are referring to what, in statistics, is called the *arithmetic mean.* There are, however, other kinds of averages, or put more formally, measures of central tendency. The most common of these are the *mode* and the *median.* We shall be looking at them in Unit 3. The calculation of the mean is straightforward. One merely sums the observations' values and then divides the total by the number of observations. For example we make eight *observations* of poor rate assessments. Each of these observations gives us a *value* (£36, £20, £20 etc). We add up these values (£195) and divide by the number of observations, which was eight.

these voters. Because our population has only eight members we do not need to sample, we can make the calculation direct: it is, as we have seen, £24¾. However, in order to demonstrate something of the principles of sampling, we are going to imagine that the population is really very much bigger and we are obliged to sample. To make the exercise easier still we're going to *round up or down* the rateable values to the nearest ten. We begin then with the position as in Table 1. In this table we have identified each name with a letter and it is these letters we shall use from now on.

We shall adopt the convention that numbers 1, 2, 3 and 4 are rounded down (ie 11, 12, 13 or 14 would appear as 10) and numbers 5, 6, 7, 8 or 9 are rounded up.

Table 1 Rateable value of property held by eight Tite voters

Identifier	Name	Rateable value
A	William Abraham	£40
B	Henry Adams	£20
C	Thomas Adams	£20
D	Hilar Aicher	£20
E	Charles Ainsworth	£30
F	James Aldous	£40
G	Charles Allen	£10
H	Francis Thomas Allen	£20
	Total	£200
	Mean value	£25

We begin with our eight voters. Let us suppose we decide to draw a sample of one. We can draw this in eight different ways as in Table 2.

Table 2 Sampling distribution of the mean of a sample of size 1 from a population of size 8

Sample no.	1	2	3	4	5	6	7	8
Sample member	A	B	C	D	E	F	G	H
Sample value (£s)	40	20	20	20	30	40	10	20
Mean value (arrived at by ÷ 1)	40	20	20	20	30	40	10	20

We can represent these samples in the form of a *histogram* as in Figure 7. The table and the figure show that if indeed we took a sample of one, we should have a wide range of mean values: from £10 to £40. We can conclude then that, in this case, taking

Or bar chart. For how to draw these, and the distinction between them, see Floud 1973 pp 51-4. The question of nominal, ordinal and interval data is dealt with in Unit 3.

Figure 7 Sampling distribution of the mean of a sample of size 1 from a population of size 8

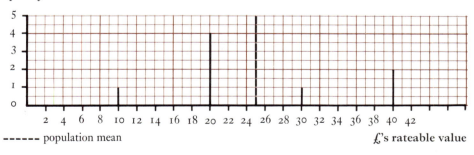

frequency

------ population mean   £'s rateable value

one sample of one did not help us much to estimate the mean *of the population*: hardly a surprising conclusion. But let us now take a sample of two. With a population of size eight we can take twenty-eight different samples of size two. If we do this we know that whatever random sample of two we might take would be included among these twenty-eight. The calculation which appears in Table 3 and Figure 8 shows the distribution of the twenty-eight means.

Table 3 Sampling distribution of the mean of a sample of size 2 from a population of size 8

Sample no.	1	2	3	4	5	6	7	8	9	10	11	12	13	14	15	16	17	18	19	20	21	22	23	24	25	26	27	28
Members of sample	A	A	A	A	A	A	A	B	B	B	B	B	B	C	C	C	C	C	D	D	D	D	E	E	E	F	F	G
	B	C	D	E	F	G	H	C	D	E	F	G	H	D	E	F	G	H	E	F	G	H	F	G	H	G	H	H
Values in sample	40	40	40	40	40	40	40	20	20	20	20	20	20	20	20	20	20	20	20	20	20	20	30	30	30	40	40	10
	20	20	20	30	40	10	20	20	20	30	40	10	20	20	30	40	10	20	30	40	10	20	40	10	20	10	20	20
Total	60	60	60	70	80	50	60	40	40	50	60	30	40	40	50	60	30	40	50	60	30	40	70	40	50	50	60	30
Mean (÷ 2)	30	30	30	35	40	25	30	20	20	25	30	15	20	20	25	30	15	20	25	30	15	20	35	20	25	25	30	15

Table 4 Sampling distribution of the mean of a sample of size 3 from a population of size 8

Sample no.	1	2	3	4	5	6	7	8	9	10	11	12	13	14	15	16	17	18	19	20	21	22	23	24	25	26	27	28
Members of sample	A	A	A	A	A	A	A	A	A	A	A	A	A	A	A	A	A	A	A	A	A	B	B	B	B	B	B	B
	B	B	B	B	B	B	C	C	C	C	C	D	D	D	D	E	E	E	F	F	G	C	C	C	C	C	D	D
	C	D	E	F	G	H	D	E	F	G	H	E	F	G	H	F	G	H	G	H	H	D	E	F	G	H	E	F
Values in sample	40	40	40	40	40	40	40	40	40	40	40	40	40	40	40	40	40	40	40	40	40	20	20	20	20	20	20	20
	20	20	20	20	20	20	20	20	20	20	20	20	20	20	20	30	30	30	40	40	10	20	20	20	20	20	20	20
	20	20	30	40	10	20	20	30	40	10	20	30	40	10	20	40	10	20	10	20	20	20	30	40	10	20	30	40
Total	80	80	90	100	70	80	80	90	100	70	80	90	100	70	80	110	80	90	90	100	70	60	70	80	50	60	70	80
Mean (÷ 3)	27	27	30	33	23	27	27	30	33	23	27	30	33	23	27	37	27	30	30	33	23	20	23	27	17	20	23	27

Sample no.	29	30	31	32	33	34	35	36	37	38	39	40	41	42	43	44	45	46	47	48	49	50	51	52	53	54	55	56
Members of sample	B	B	B	B	B	B	B	B	C	C	C	C	C	C	C	C	C	C	D	D	D	D	D	D	E	E	E	F
	D	D	E	E	E	F	F	G	D	D	D	D	E	E	E	F	F	G	E	E	E	F	F	G	F	F	G	G
	G	H	F	G	H	G	H	H	E	F	G	H	F	G	H	G	H	H	F	G	H	G	H	H	G	H	H	H
Values in sample	20	20	20	20	20	20	20	20	20	20	20	20	20	20	20	20	20	20	20	20	20	20	20	20	30	30	30	40
	20	20	30	30	30	40	40	10	20	20	20	20	30	30	30	40	40	10	30	30	30	40	40	10	40	40	10	10
	10	20	40	10	20	10	20	20	30	40	10	20	40	10	20	10	20	20	40	10	20	10	20	20	10	20	20	20
Total	50	60	90	60	70	70	80	50	70	80	50	60	90	60	70	70	80	50	90	60	70	70	80	50	80	90	60	70
Mean (÷3)	17	20	30	20	23	23	27	17	23	27	17	20	30	20	23	23	27	17	30	20	23	23	27	17	27	30	20	23

Figure 8 Sampling distribution of the mean of a sample of size 2 from a population of size 8

frequency

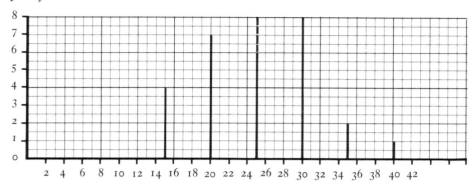

£'s rateable value

Table 3 and Figure 8 show that when the sample size is increased to two, the mean of many of the samples moves closer to the population mean. Thus, with a sample size of one (Table 2), five of the eight sample means were within £5 of the population mean (ie there were four of £20 each and one of £30). When we increase the sample size to two, however, we find that twenty-one out of twenty-eight sample means were within £5 of the population mean, ie three out of four.

Let us now increase our sample size to three. The results of this exercise appear in Table 4 and Figure 9.

They reveal that now forty-four out of fifty-six of our sample means are within £5 of the population mean. You will also note that the extreme means (ie the six at £17 and the one on £37) are also now closer to the population mean than when our sample size was two or one.

We will now take one more sample before we quit. The arithmetical labour is getting too much! This time our sample size is four. The results appear in Table 5 and Figure 10.

Table 5 and Figure 10 continue the trend noticed earlier. Now of the seventy

Figure 9 Sampling distribution of the mean of a sample of size 3 from a population of size 8

frequency

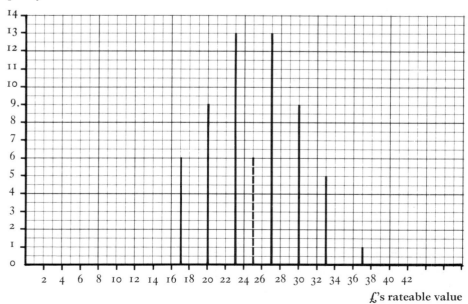

£'s rateable value

Table 5 Sampling distribution of the mean of a sample of size 4 from a population of size 8

Sample no.	1	2	3	4	5	6	7	8	9	10	11	12	13	14	15	16	17	18	19	20	21	22	23
Members of sample	A	A	A	A	A	A	A	A	A	A	A	A	A	A	A	A	A	A	A	A	A	A	A
	B	B	B	B	B	B	B	B	B	B	B	B	B	B	B	C	C	C	C	C	C	C	C
	C	C	C	C	C	D	D	D	D	E	E	E	F	F	G	D	D	D	D	E	E	E	F
	D	E	F	G	H	E	F	G	H	F	G	H	G	H	H	E	F	G	H	F	G	H	G
Values in sample	40	40	40	40	40	40	40	40	40	40	40	40	40	40	40	40	40	40	40	40	40	40	40
	20	20	20	20	20	20	20	20	20	20	20	20	20	20	20	20	20	20	20	20	20	20	20
	20	20	20	20	20	20	20	20	20	30	30	30	40	40	10	20	20	20	20	30	30	30	40
	20	30	40	10	20	30	40	10	20	40	10	20	10	20	20	30	40	10	20	40	10	20	10
Total	100	110	120	90	100	110	120	90	100	130	100	110	110	120	90	110	120	90	100	130	100	110	110
Mean (÷ 4)	25	28	30	23	25	28	30	23	25	33	25	28	28	30	23	28	30	23	25	33	25	28	28

Sample no.	24	25	26	27	28	29	30	31	32	33	34	35	36	37	38	39	40	41	42	43	44	45	46
Members of sample	A	A	A	A	A	A	A	A	A	A	A	A	B	B	B	B	B	B	B	B	B	B	B
	C	C	D	D	D	D	D	D	E	E	E	F	C	C	C	C	C	C	C	C	C	C	D
	F	G	E	E	E	F	F	G	F	F	G	G	D	D	D	D	E	E	E	F	F	G	E
	H	H	F	G	H	G	H	H	G	H	H	H	E	F	G	H	F	G	H	G	H	H	F
Values in sample	40	40	40	40	40	40	40	40	40	40	40	40	20	20	20	20	20	20	20	20	20	20	20
	20	20	20	20	20	20	20	20	30	30	30	40	20	20	20	20	20	20	20	20	20	20	20
	40	10	30	30	30	40	40	10	40	40	10	10	20	20	20	20	30	30	30	40	40	10	30
	20	20	40	10	20	10	20	20	10	20	20	20	30	40	10	20	40	10	20	10	20	20	40
Total	120	90	130	100	110	110	120	90	120	130	100	110	90	100	70	80	110	80	90	90	100	70	110
Mean (÷ 4)	30	23	33	25	28	28	30	23	30	33	25	28	23	25	18	20	28	20	23	23	25	18	28

Sample no.	47	48	49	50	51	52	53	54	55	56	57	58	59	60	61	62	63	64	65	66	67	68	69	70
Members of sample	B	B	B	B	B	B	B	B	B	C	C	C	C	C	C	C	C	C	C	D	D	D	D	E
	D	D	D	D	D	E	E	E	F	D	D	D	D	D	D	E	E	E	F	E	E	E	F	F
	E	E	F	F	G	F	F	G	G	E	E	E	F	F	G	F	F	G	G	F	F	G	G	G
	G	H	G	H	H	G	H	H	H	F	G	H	G	H	H	G	H	H	H	G	H	H	H	H
Values in sample	20	20	20	20	20	20	20	20	20	20	20	20	20	20	20	20	20	20	20	20	20	20	20	30
	20	20	20	20	20	30	30	30	40	20	20	20	20	20	20	30	30	30	40	30	30	30	40	40
	30	30	40	40	10	40	40	10	10	30	30	30	40	40	10	40	40	10	10	40	40	10	10	10
	10	20	10	20	20	10	20	20	20	40	10	20	10	20	20	10	20	20	20	10	20	20	20	20
Total	80	90	90	100	70	100	110	80	90	110	80	90	90	100	70	100	110	80	90	100	110	80	90	100
Mean (÷ 4)	20	23	23	25	18	25	28	20	23	28	20	23	23	25	18	25	28	20	23	25	28	20	23	25

Figure 10 Sampling distribution of the mean of a sample of size 4 from a population of size 8

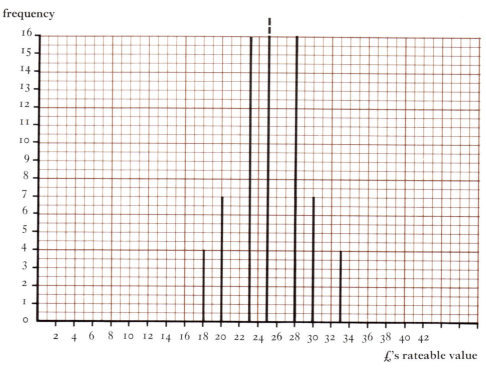

sample means, as many as sixty-two are within £5 of the population mean and the extremes (the four means of £18 and the four of £33) are closer to the population mean than the extreme values in our sample of three. Another point to notice is that the histogram in Figure 10 (representing the sample means) is very nearly symmetrical around the population mean. Indeed, as we have increased the size of our sample, the more symmetrical have the collection of histograms become, as well as moving closer to the population mean. They have in fact approached the shape that appears in Figure 11 and is called by statisticians the *normal curve*, or more fully the *normal distribution curve*.

To grasp a little more of this, let us turn again to our findings. In Table 6 we have summarized those findings. Let us focus our attention on the last line of the table, the one indicating the position when we drew samples of four from our population of eight. The table shows that in eighty-nine per cent of our samples the sample mean fell within £5 either side of the population mean of £25. But how confident can we be that a single randomly chosen sample will be one whose mean value lies within £5 of the population mean? The answer to this is that there is for the population we are considering a sixty-two to seventy chance that it does. Or to put it in percentage terms, eighty-nine per cent of our samples would have means falling within this interval: and eleven per cent would be outside it. In other words we can be eighty-nine

Table 6 Number of samples whose mean values fall within £5 and £10 of the population mean of £25, with samples of size 1–4

Sample size	Sample means in the range	
	£20–£30	£15–£35
1	63% ($\frac{5}{8}$)	63% ($\frac{5}{8}$)
2	75% ($\frac{21}{28}$)	96% ($\frac{27}{28}$)
3	79% ($\frac{44}{56}$)	98% ($\frac{55}{56}$)
4	89% ($\frac{62}{70}$)	100% ($\frac{70}{70}$)

Figure 11 Normal curve

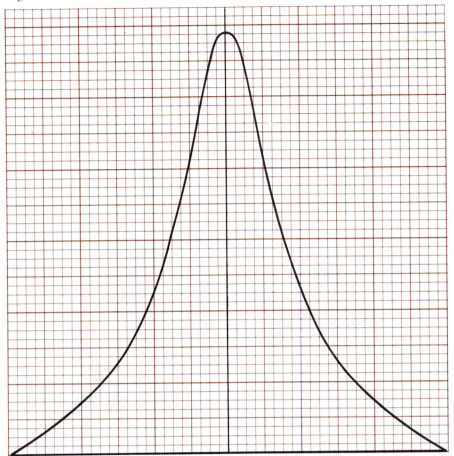

per cent confident that the mean of a randomly chosen sample will lie within £5 of the population mean. That means, in this particular case, it will lie between £20 and £30.

But suppose we want to know the chance of the mean of a random sample falling within £10 either way (plus or minus) of the population mean: in other words lying somewhere between £15 and £35. In our particular case by choosing a sample of four from a population of eight, each possible sample mean is certain to lie in this interval. Put another way, the chance that a sample mean will lie within a certain symmetrical interval drawn about the population mean will increase with the width of the interval.

You will also notice from Table 6 that the chance that the mean of a randomly chosen sample will lie within, say, £5 of the population mean will depend upon the size of sample selected. For an arbitrarily defined interval, the chance that the mean of a randomly chosen sample will lie within it will be greater for larger samples, ie say for samples of four than for samples of three or two.

We can now go no further in this empirical manner. But before turning to the next unit, let us summarize what our somewhat tortuous progress seems to suggest:

1 If we want to discover, *precisely*, the mean of a set of values of a characteristic of some population, the only way we can do so is to examine every single member of the population and subject it to the appropriate mathematical treatment.

2 If, however, we are content with an *estimate* of the mean (or any other parameter for that matter) we can find this by taking a *random sample* of the population.

3 We must be careful to ensure that the sample is random. If it is distorted in any way we are unlikely to be able to make a satisfactory estimate of the parameter of the population we are seeking.

Figure 12

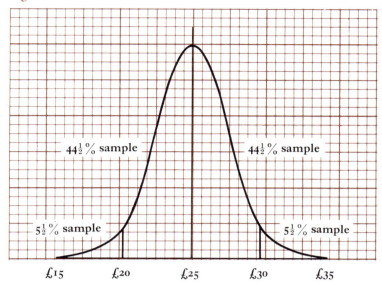

| £15 | £20 | £25 | £30 | £35 |

4 Our laboriously worked out example has suggested that as we increase the size of our sample, the pattern of the histograms, representing the frequencies of the means of the same value, will tend towards a shape approximating to that of a normal curve.

5 Some of the samples will have means that are closer to the population mean than will others. In our illustration we could represent the situation as in Figure 12. This shows the proportion of sample means falling within certain intervals drawn symmetrically around the population mean.

6 Figure 12 also gives us the situation as occurred when our sample size was four. With this sample size we found that eighty-nine per cent of our sample means fall within £5 of the population mean.

7 Figure 12 also shows that if we increase the interval in which our sample means may fall, say to $\pm$ £10 of the population mean (in other words if we are prepared to accept a less precise estimate of the population mean), then we can be certain, in this case one hundred per cent certain, that all the sample means will fall within it.

8 One final point, if we are prepared to put up with a situation where only ninety-two per cent of our sample means will fall within £10 either side ($\pm$ £10) of the population mean then we need only take a random sample of two (see Table 6). In this case eight per cent of our sample means would lie outside this particular interval: just as with a sample size of four and an interval of $\pm$ £5, eleven per cent of the sample means would lie outside. But this is a price we have to pay. It is part of the process of sampling and is called *sample error* or *sampling variability*. It is not to be confused with *sample bias*. The latter is due to mistakes made in drawing the sample and can be avoided: the former is part and parcel of the mathematics of sampling and is always present and though it can be reduced, cannot be avoided altogether.

4 Some self-assessment questions in sampling

SAQ 1 Turn to the *Bath Poll Book* of 1855 and draw up a table of the first eight of Whateley's voters along the same lines as Table 1 above.

SAQ 2 Draw histograms to represent sampling distributions of the mean rateable value of the first eight of Whateley's voters (Bath election 1855), with a sample size of 1, 2, 3 and 4. In other words, do for the first eight of Whateley's voters what I did above for Tite's.

SAQ 3 As sample size increases, the distribution of the means becomes more symmetrical and less dispersed. What difference, in this regard, do you notice between the distributions, at respective sample sizes, of Tite's and Whateley's voters.

SAQ 4 Draw up a table for Whateley's voters along the lines of Table 6. When you have done so answer the following questions:
1 What (in £s) are the upper and lower limits of the two intervals in your table?
2 How confident can you be (in percentage terms) that with a sample size of 4 any one of your sample means will lie within ± £5 of the population mean?
3 How confident can you be (in percentage terms) that with a sample size of 4 any one of your sample means will lie within ± £10 of the population mean?

SAQ 5 The answers to SAQ 3 show that at any sample size we can be less confident that our sample means will lie within ± £5 or ± £10 of the population mean than in the case of Tite's voters. Give one reason to account for this. For a clue see my mother's method of buying tomatoes (p 35).

SAQ 6 It has been suggested that I failed in Unit 1 to take into account the considerable changes that have taken place in the teaching of history over the past couple of decades. You may remember that I alleged that 'the historian's early fare is still that which produced the sort of questions which . . . I attempted to answer some twenty years ago' (p 13). How would *you* discover whether I am right or wrong?
1 Ask a historian.
2 Ask two historians.
3 Ask 100 historians.
4 Make an analysis of history books published over the last twenty years.
5 Classify all the questions asked of aspirants for Oxford and Cambridge scholarships over the last twenty years according to whether they: *a* were couched in terms of 'named individuals', *b* dealt with 'constitutional, governmental or party political matters', or *c* were 'cliché-ridden'.
6 Classify *all* the questions asked in *all* the history papers set by *all* the General Certificate of Education Examination Boards at Advanced and Scholarship level in each year 1953–73.
7 Some other method.

SAQ 7 Having decided to draw a sample of questions from the GCE Advanced and Scholarship papers of the last twenty years, how would you produce your sampling frame?
1 Make a list of all the Examining Boards, draw a sample from it and then sample all the questions asked by those Boards.
2 Make a list of all the history papers set over the past twenty years, draw a sample from that, and then analyse all the questions asked in each paper.
3 Make a list of all the questions asked in each of the history papers and draw a sample from that.

SAQ 8 Having decided to draw a sample of questions directly, would you:
1 Draw a random sample?
2 Draw a systematic sample, say every tenth question from your list?
If you are thinking of choosing solution 2 look back at the example of systematic sampling given on pp 42–3 and then think for a moment or two about the layout of examination questions in history papers.

SAQ 9 Draw a random sample of 200 Whateley votes. Begin to draw the sample at the top left-hand corner of the second page of the Table of Random Sampling

Numbers, and proceed downwards, ie begin with 1616 and go to 9863 : 0103 : 2907 etc. If you come across the same number twice, ignore it and move on to the next one. Do not forget to use the 'short cut' method (see p 42). Put a mark against each name you draw. You don't need to make a separate list, but you can if you find this convenient. Check the time, to see how long this exercise takes you. When you have your 200 votes work out the mean of the rateable values.

SAQ 10 Draw a systematic sample from the list of persons who voted for Whateley, or Tite or who did not vote. Go through the lists taking every fifth name, ie in the case of Whateley voters your first three names should be William Abbott, William Alexander and John Thos Anstey.

 Make a separate list of rateable values for each (Whateley : Tite : non-voters) and work out the mean rateable value for each. From the summary table at the end of the poll book work out the mean rateable value for the three populations (Whateley : Tite : non-voters) and compare each of these three parameters with the respective statistics for your samples. What do you notice about the comparisons ?

SAQ 11 You will have noticed that the systematic sample of Whateley voters produced a mean rateable value of $£54\frac{1}{10}$ which was closer to the population mean of $£54\frac{4}{10}$ than was the random sample value of $£50\frac{1}{4}$. Why should this be so ?
a Because systematic sampling is more accurate than random sampling ?
or
b Because of sampling error ?

SAQ 12 The mean rateable value of the sample of 102 non-voters at $£46\frac{1}{2}$ was very close to the population value of $£47\frac{6}{10}$. Had you not known the population means for Whateley, Tite or the non-voters, would your confidence in this statistic have been the same as the confidence you had in the corresponding statistic for Whateley and Tite. Would it have been more or would it have been less ?

SAQ 13 How would you draw a sample of the non-voters so you could have the same confidence in any statistics derived from it as from the samples of Whateley's and Tite's voters ?

Answers to SAQs

Answer SAQ 1

Rateable value of property held by eight Whateley voters

Identifier	Name	Rateable value
A	William Abbott	£50
B	George Abraham	£30
C	Edward H. Acton	£60
D	George Adams	£60
E	Robert Alexander	£30
F	William Alexander	£80
G	John Allen	£20
H	William Proctor Anderdon	£110
	Total	£440
	Mean	£55

Answer SAQ 2

Whateley's votes: sampling distribution of the mean of a sample of size 1 from a population of size 8

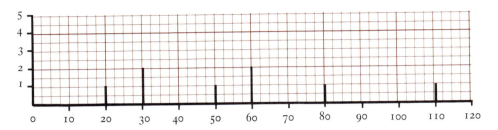

Whateley's votes: sampling distribution of the mean of a sample of size 2 from a population of size 8

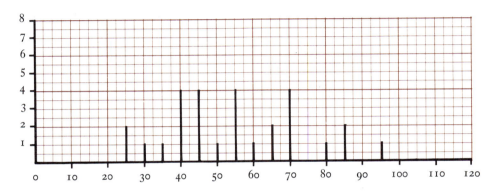

Whateley's votes: sampling distribution of the mean of a sample of size 3 from a population of size 8

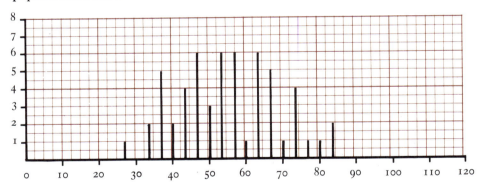

Whateley's votes: sampling distribution of the mean of a sample of size 4 from a population of size 8

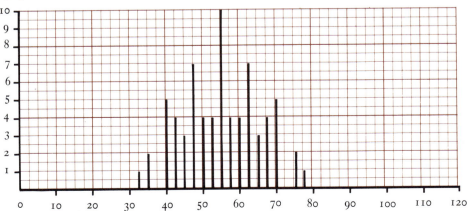

Answer SAQ 3   The distributions of the rateable values of Whateley's voters are not as symmetrical as Tite's. Also the dispersion or spread is greater.

Answer SAQ 4   Number of samples whose mean values fall within £5 and £10 of the population mean of £55, with samples of size 1–4.

Sample size	Sample means in the interval	
	£50–£60	£45–£65
1	38% ($\frac{3}{8}$)	38% ($\frac{3}{8}$)
2	21% ($\frac{6}{28}$)	43% ($\frac{12}{28}$)
3	29% ($\frac{16}{56}$)	50% ($\frac{28}{56}$)
4	40% ($\frac{28}{70}$)	69% ($\frac{48}{70}$)

1 £50–£60 : £45–£65
2 40 per cent
3 69 per cent

Answer SAQ 5   So far as rateable values are concerned, Tite's voters were a much more homogeneous bunch than were Whateley's. You will see that the former's ranged from £10 to £40 and that though the population size was eight, there were only four values (£10, £20, £30 and £40). In the case of Whateley, on the other hand, the values ranged from £20 to £110, and there were seven different values among the eight observations. It is not difficult to appreciate that when the values of a population vary widely, drawing a sample of any given size to represent that population closely is going to be more difficult (or, to put it another way, less likely) than when the values vary narrowly. This is brought out when we look at the samples drawn from Tite's and Whateley's voters. In all sampling we must estimate how variable the population is before we can decide how confident we can be of any conclusions we draw from it. You will notice, by the way, if you compare Table 6 and the table given in the answer to SAQ 4 that one can overcome, to some extent, the problem of the variability of Whateley's voters (as compared to Tite's) by increasing the sample size of the former.

We must pause here, since to calculate this 'variability factor', is not to be attempted in this unit. It will be done in Unit 3 – on page 87 for those who cannot wait till next week!

Answer SAQ 6   I hope you will agree that we are unlikely to get very near the truth, or at least we won't know whether we are near it or not, if we adopt solutions 1 or 2. Even solution 3 would be impressionistic and we would have to decide first on how to select our 100 historians and second on what they based their answers. Solution 4 would involve us in trying to determine which history books published during the last twenty years were read by budding historians, which reached them via their teachers (and what happened to their findings during this process) and finally, what books had no impact at all. Also, one should perhaps not confine one's attention to books, but should also include journals. Solution 5 seems to me to be getting nearer to the answer, but this might be my Oxbridge *bias*! It is true that many professional historians are trained at Cambridge or Oxford and that many spend their tender and not so tender years training, as it were, for the Open Scholarship examinations. I once knew a History Fellow of King's College, Cambridge, who confided in me that from the age of fourteen he did virtually nothing else! However, it is obviously not true that all historians in England are products of Oxford and Cambridge and, therefore, this particular examination may not represent the 'early fare' I talked about. Solution 6 would seem to widen the population in an appropriate manner. The problem here, of course, is that it does so to an inordinate extent. I haven't attempted to discover how many questions have been set over the past twenty years, but I imagine it must run into tens of thousands. It is for this reason that I would look to solution 7 and seek some other method. No great wit is required to guess that I would choose to *sample* GCE Advanced and Scholarship papers in history.

Answer SAQ 7   If you choose to adopt either solution 1 or solution 2 you would be conducting an exercise in *cluster* sampling. This is an understandable technique to adopt in the circumstances, since it obviously saves a lot of time, but it has its drawbacks. This is because by sampling Examination Boards (solution 1) or examination papers (solution 2) you are only indirectly sampling examination questions. And it is the latter you are really after. Each Board produces annually a *cluster* of papers, and each paper contains a *cluster* of questions. Now it is widely known, for example, that Boards vary considerably in the kind of papers they set. It could well be, therefore, that in sampling Boards, or papers, rather than questions, one is getting an unrepresentative sample of the questions set across the country as a whole. Questions within a paper, or papers within a Board's domain will be comparatively homogeneous. Between Boards and between papers there is likely to be considerable variability. What to do about this poses a considerable problem which goes beyond the scope of this unit. We shall, however, be discussing cluster sampling on radio programme one, *Sampling Historical Data*. To sum up, if at all possible, one should attempt to sample questions directly and, therefore, one's sampling frame should consist of all the questions set.

Answer SAQ 8   I think solution 1 is the safest, principally because the questions in history papers are traditionally ordered in a chronological fashion. Any form of systematic sampling may then bias the sample towards say questions on medieval history, or eighteenth-century history and these or any other periods may have particular characteristics not found to the same degree elsewhere.

Answer SAQ 9   I calculated the mean rateable value of my 200 Whateley voters to be $£49\frac{4}{10}$. It took me $2\frac{1}{2}$ hours to complete the calculation. I hope you persevered with this exercise not because I am a sadist but because this kind of tedious work is something you may well come across in your project and it is important to get the feel of it. It is also important for you to begin to get some idea of how long various research procedures take *you*, so that when embarking on your own research project you will have some idea of how long it is going to take. Incidentally in this particular case you might be thinking that the difference between the time it took you to take a sample of 200 and do the calculation and the time it would have taken you to treat the whole population was probably not very great. And, as we have seen, our sample statistic is $£49\frac{4}{10}$ which you may think is rather a long way from the population parameter of $£54\frac{4}{10}$. The point to note here, however, is that had the population been 11,260,000 instead of 1,126 you could have taken a random sample of 200 and been just as confident as to how close its mean would be to the population mean. The reason is that what determines the accuracy of the sample is the *absolute* size of the sample and not its size relative to that of the population.

Random sample of 200 Whateley voters

	X		X
1		Henry Rawlings	£35
Christopher Brickman	£36	John Isles	£12
Thomas Spiller	£30	Charles Chislett	£28
William Roach Wood	£15	Charles Edward Davis	£48
Edward Briscoe	£48	William Stockalm	£27
Charles Cockle	£22		
Joseph Walker	£60	**61**	
William Rainey	£20	John Wiltshire	£45
James Pocock	£40	(Miss out Thomas Barrett)	
Thomas Manning	£25	William Cooper	£20
William Duffield	£50	William Burridge	£17
		John North	£25
11		William Payne	£25
John Hawkins	£16	William Clement	£85
William Simpson	£70	Charles Book	£17
Thomas Catley	£26	Samuel Say	£11
George Powell	£62	(Miss out Thomas Feltham Packer)	
William Eversley	£47	George Wigens	£25
Thomas Augustus Strong	£20	(Miss out Samuel George Mitchell)	
John Howe	£40	Henry Dummett	£70
John Taylor	£196		
William Lindsay	£45	**71**	
Richard Feakins	£80	John Hulbert	£60
		Gideon Ball	£55
21		(Miss out George Wigens)	
John Veal	£21	Henry Thomas Jennings	£105
John Graham	£20	John Tylee	£40
Joseph Dunscombe	£16	William Sibley	£45
James Parsons	£16	William Williamson	£12
William Phipps	£156	James Howell	£10
Thomas Barrett	£60	Daniel Weller	£70
John Shaul	£20	Joseph Broadhurst	£42
Isaac Nowell	£40	Henry Higgins	£25
John Howes	£30		
Henry Lawson	£110	**81**	
		John Luce Barfoot	£35
31		Francis Baynes Wright	£75
John Milton Tayler	£65	George Newman	£117
Abel Andrew Straghan	£40	Richard Rudman	£20
Benjamin Bartrum	£146	John Morris	£40
William Clarke	£28	Alfred Mason	£30
Colin Mackenzie	£72	Samuel Rogers jnr.	£20
Charles Crowden	£16	William Targett	£24
George Williams	£108	Edmund Lloyd Bagshawe	£65
William Jones	£66	Robert Robertson	£165
Samuel George Mitchell	£45		
Thomas Feltham Packer	£75	**91**	
		William Robertson	£50
41		William Roper	£34
Henry Singer	£25	James Austin	£22
Thomas Marrett	£70	Douglas Cox	£25
Thomas Edward Marsh	£42	William Bird	£18
John Snook	£24	John Johnson	£123
James Limbrick	£85	(Miss out Henry Rawlings)	
James Bourn	£60	Fountayne Elwin	£60
George East	£30	John Saunders	£65
Richard Ford	£50	Edward Fitzgerald	£135
William Seymour	£55	William Budge	£23
John Whittaker	£50		
		101	
51		Jas. Carpenter Pearks	£24
William Tanner	£14	Charles Wolfe	£14
Thomas Butcher	£132	John Comber	£10
James Robbins	£22	Richard Hancock	£75
(Miss out William Phipps)		Richard Thomas Gore	£70
George Field	£70	William Stowell	£24
Samuel Turner	£50		

	X		X
Joseph Cockle	£10	William Hancock	£40
George King	£55	(Miss out Thomas Mundy)	
William Hunt	£75	Matthew Parker	£80
Edward Benjamin Bagshawe	£70	James Mans	£19
		James Gardiner	£30
III		George Leighton Wood	£131
Robert Brooks Arnold	£75	George Mackillop	£60
Walter Gibbs	£30	**161**	
Charles Target	£25	William Withers	£120
Stephen Moody	£14	Edward Hooper	£45
Charles Olds	£40	Charles Geary Meyler	£52
Frederick Bennett	£48	Francis Seymour Hamilton	£50
Edmund Wise	£10	Thomas Sawtell	£17
George Nicholas Dangerfield	£26	Paul Wilkins	£28
Benjamin Marshman	£10	Richard Parker	£20
William Dayer	£10	(Miss out William Tanner)	
		William Pond	£10
121		John Lord	£122
Thomas Baldwin	£40	Willoughby Bean	£70
Benjamin Francis Shaw	£18	**171**	
William Burns	£65	Robert Nathaniel Stone	£60
Charles Rawlings	£10	George Davis	£55
John Soden	£110	William Veale	£17
Thomas Wm Harrington	£36	William Pittard	£19
(Miss out Charles Wolfe)		George Sainsbury	£50
William Kidner Sharland	£80	Charles Jas. Mather	£15
William Hyde	£36	John Taylor	£30
Robert Walker	£19	George Hawkins	£163
John Baker	£20	William Davey	£80
		(Miss out Christopher Brickman)	
131		Henry Smith Brice	£60
John George	£30	**181**	
Francis White	£30	William March	£28
Thomas Mundy	£25	Thomas Whiddon	£27
George William Cole	£36	George Holmes	£14
John Kemp	£110	Joseph Raymond King	£90
Robert Berwick Were	£50	Walter Irvine	£55
Benjamin Smith	£10	John Lamble Harrison	£70
Isaac Bryant	£26	Henry Baker	£23
Joseph Fisher	£10	David Anthony	£47
William Seymour	£55	(Miss out George Nicholas Dangerfield)	
141		(Miss out Edward Hooper)	
Thomas Harvey	£65	Thomas Goldsborough Stockwell	£65
(Miss out William Clement)		John Perrett	£30
John Jennings	£25	**191**	
William Elliott	£63	John James	£12
James Hulbert	£32	Joseph Maggs	£10
William Henry Roberts	£94	Daniel Race Godfrey	£225
(Miss out Richard Ford)		Charles Benjamin	£40
Edmund Wilcox	£15	William Harrison	£62
Watkin Watkins	£75	(Miss out William Roper)	
William Glen Hill	£24	(Miss out Henry Lawson)	
(Miss out Henry Rawlings)		George Adams	£60
James Dolman	£150	John Bond	£55
James Chadwick	£28	William Dawson Winckworth	£52
151		(Miss out Thomas Harvey)	
John Samuel Graves	£60	Henry Thomas Gill	£12
Thomas Buckman	£16	(Miss out John Lamble Harrison)	
(Miss out Samuel Say)		Edward Gibbons	£82
John Whittaker	£169		
James Quaife Dombraine	£50		
(Miss out James Dolman)			

Mean value of random sample of Whateley voters = £49 $\frac{4}{10}$ Mean value of all Whateley voters = £54 $\frac{4}{10}$

Answer SAQ 10
Mean rateable value of 226 Whateley voters $= £54\frac{1}{10}$
Mean rateable value of **all** Whateley voters $= £54\frac{4}{10}$
Mean rateable value of 236 Tite voters $= £36$
Mean rateable value of **all** Tite voters $= £33\frac{4}{10}$
Mean rateable value of 102 non-voters $= £46\frac{1}{2}$
Mean rateable value of **all** non-voters $= £47\frac{6}{10}$

You probably noticed that you took much less time over the systematic sampling. I spent half an hour each on Whateley and Tite and twenty minutes on the non-voters.

Answer SAQ 11   Sampling error accounts for the difference. Random sampling using a table of random numbers is the most accurate method of sampling. Actually in this case because of the way the list of voters is drawn up our systematic sample is probably the same as a random one. However, as we saw with our exercises above (pp 45–51), in drawing a sample of any particular size we can only be confident that whatever statistic we are seeking will lie within a certain interval. This will be greater or smaller depending upon the size of our sample and the variability of the items within the population from which it is drawn.

Answer SAQ 12   The closeness of the result was due to chance. Had we not known the population mean value we would have had less confidence in the figure because the sample size was less than half that of Whateley's and Tite's voters and it is sample size which determines our confidence in a particular statistic (other things being equal), not the proportion it bears to the total population.

Answer SAQ 13   Increase the sample size by increasing the *sampling fraction*. For instance in this case we could take every second non-voter, not every fifth.

5 Conclusion

The aim of this unit has been to give you some idea of the power, and the limitations, of sampling. Personally I think sampling opens up very exciting prospects. By adopting sampling techniques your projects can have a much wider significance. And even if you choose not to sample an understanding of the principles underlying the technique will enable you to interpret your findings more effectively. You will be able to do this because you will be aware of how far your findings can be generalized and how far they cannot. And in this way you will be demonstrating what I think is the most important characteristic of sampling, namely the non-quantitative intellectual demands it makes upon its practitioners. We have demonstrated this in the discussion of the attempts by Bradburn and Berlew to draw an appropriate sample of English literature and in our attempt to decide the question of what fare budding historians were being fed today and over the past twenty years. To coin a phrase – again – sampling is too important to be left to the statisticians.

Figure 13: Map showing location of parishes analysed for the Cambridge Group for the History of Population and Social Structure. The map also shows the location of a random sample of parishes. Discussed in radio programme *Sampling Historical Data*.

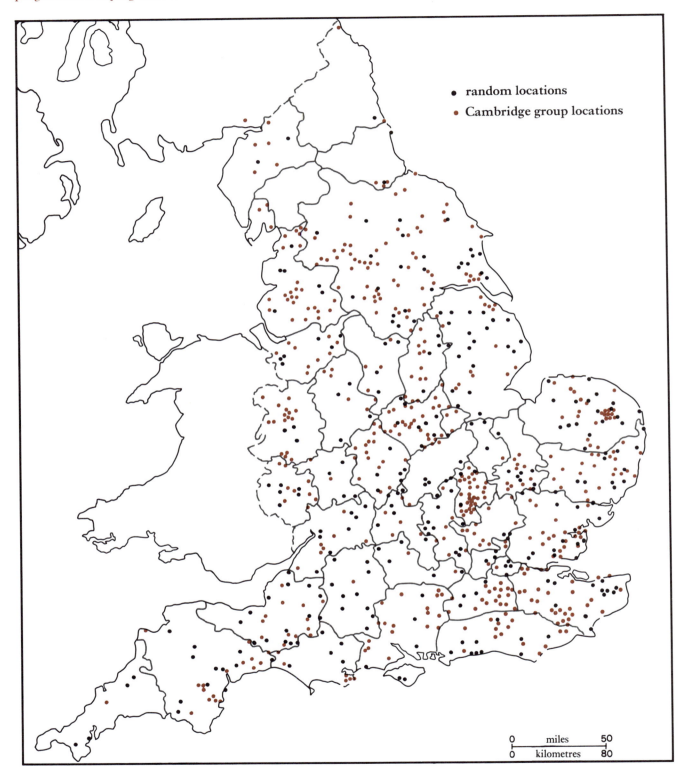

Appendix   Table of random sampling numbers*

```
20 17   42 28   23 17   59 66   38 61   02 10   86 10   51 55   92 52   44 25
74 49   04 49   03 04   10 33   53 70   11 54   48 63   94 60   94 49   57 38
94 70   49 31   38 67   23 42   29 65   40 88   78 71   37 18   48 64   06 57
22 15   78 15   69 84   32 52   32 54   15 12   54 02   01 37   38 37   12 93
93 29   12 18   27 30   30 55   91 87   50 57   58 51   49 36   12 53   96 40

45 04   77 97   36 14   99 45   52 95   69 85   03 83   51 87   85 56   22 37
44 91   99 49   89 39   94 60   48 49   06 77   64 72   59 26   08 51   25 57
16 23   91 02   19 96   47 59   89 65   27 84   30 92   63 37   26 24   23 66
04 50   65 04   65 65   82 42   70 51   55 04   61 47   88 83   99 34   82 37
32 70   17 72   03 61   66 26   24 71   22 77   88 33   17 78   08 92   73 49

03 64   59 07   42 95   81 39   06 41   20 81   92 34   51 90   39 08   21 42
62 49   00 90   67 86   93 48   31 83   19 07   67 68   49 03   27 47   52 03
61 00   95 86   98 36   14 03   48 88   51 07   33 40   06 86   33 76   68 57
89 03   90 49   28 74   21 04   09 96   60 45   22 03   52 80   01 79   33 81
01 72   33 85   52 40   60 07   06 71   89 27   14 29   55 24   85 79   31 96

27 56   49 79   34 34   32 22   60 53   91 17   33 26   44 70   93 14   99 70
49 05   74 48   10 55   35 25   24 28   20 22   35 66   66 34   26 35   91 23
49 74   37 25   97 26   33 94   42 23   01 28   59 58   92 69   03 66   73 82
20 26   22 43   88 08   19 85   08 12   47 65   65 63   56 07   97 85   56 79
48 87   77 96   43 39   76 93   08 79   22 18   54 55   93 75   97 26   90 77

08 72   87 46   75 73   00 11   27 07   05 20   30 85   22 21   04 67   19 13
95 97   98 62   17 27   31 42   64 71   46 22   32 75   19 32   20 99   94 85
37 99   57 31   70 40   46 55   46 12   24 32   36 74   69 20   72 10   95 93
05 79   58 37   85 33   75 18   88 71   23 44   54 28   00 48   96 23   66 45
55 85   63 42   00 79   91 22   29 01   41 39   51 40   36 65   26 11   78 32

67 28   96 25   68 36   24 72   03 85   49 24   05 69   64 86   08 19   91 21
85 86   94 78   32 59   51 82   86 43   73 84   45 60   89 57   06 87   08 15
40 10   60 09   05 88   78 44   63 13   58 25   37 11   18 47   75 62   52 21
94 55   89 48   90 80   77 80   26 89   87 44   23 74   66 20   20 19   26 52
11 63   77 77   23 20   33 62   62 19   29 03   94 15   56 37   14 09   47 16

64 00   26 04   54 55   38 57   94 62   68 40   26 04   24 25   03 61   01 20
50 94   13 23   78 41   60 58   10 60   88 46   30 21   45 98   70 96   36 89
66 98   37 96   44 13   45 05   34 59   75 85   48 97   27 19   17 85   48 51
66 91   42 83   60 77   90 91   60 90   79 62   57 66   72 28   08 70   96 03
33 58   12 18   02 07   19 40   21 29   39 45   90 42   58 84   85 43   95 67

52 49   40 16   72 40   73 05   50 90   02 04   98 24   05 30   27 25   20 88
74 98   93 99   78 30   79 47   96 92   45 58   40 37   89 76   84 41   74 68
50 26   54 30   01 88   69 57   54 45   69 88   23 21   05 69   93 44   05 32
49 46   61 89   33 79   96 84   28 34   19 35   28 73   39 59   56 34   97 07
19 65   13 44   78 39   73 88   62 03   36 00   25 96   86 76   67 90   21 68

64 17   47 67   87 59   81 40   72 61   14 00   28 28   55 86   23 38   16 15
18 43   97 37   68 97   56 56   57 95   01 88   11 89   48 07   42 60   11 92
65 58   60 87   51 09   96 61   15 53   66 81   66 88   44 75   37 01   28 88
79 90   31 00   91 14   85 65   31 75   43 15   45 93   64 78   34 53   88 02
07 23   00 15   59 05   16 09   94 42   20 40   63 76   65 67   34 11   94 10

90 08   14 24   01 51   95 46   30 32   33 19   00 14   19 28   40 51   92 69
53 82   62 02   21 82   34 13   41 03   12 85   65 30   00 97   56 30   15 48
98 17   26 15   04 50   76 25   20 33   54 84   39 31   23 33   59 64   96 27
08 91   12 44   82 40   30 62   45 50   64 54   65 17   89 25   59 44   99 95
37 21   46 77   84 87   67 39   85 54   97 37   33 41   11 74   90 50   29 62
```

Each digit is an independent sample from a population in which the digits 0 to 9 are equally likely, that is each has a probability of $\frac{1}{10}$.

* Source: D. V. Lindley and J. C. P. Miller (1968) *Cambridge Elementary Statistical Tables*, Cambridge, Cambridge University Press, pp 12–13.

16 16	57 04	81 71	17 46	53 29	73 46	42 73	77 63	62 58	60 59
98 63	89 52	77 23	61 08	63 90	80 38	42 71	85 70	04 81	05 50
01 03	09 35	02 54	51 96	92 75	58 29	24 23	25 19	89 97	91 29
29 07	16 34	49 22	52 96	89 34	17 11	06 91	24 38	55 06	83 59
72 61	80 54	70 99	24 64	11 38	83 65	27 23	40 37	84 58	48 53
71 11	41 82	79 37	00 45	98 54	52 89	26 34	40 13	60 38	08 86
61 05	66 18	76 82	11 18	61 90	90 63	78 57	32 06	39 95	75 94
81 89	42 34	00 49	97 53	33 16	26 91	57 58	42 48	51 05	48 27
10 24	90 84	22 16	26 96	54 11	01 96	58 81	37 97	80 98	72 81
14 28	33 43	01 32	58 39	19 54	56 57	23 58	24 87	77 36	20 97
35 41	17 89	87 04	28 32	13 45	59 03	91 08	69 24	84 44	42 83
07 89	36 87	98 73	77 64	75 19	05 61	11 64	31 75	49 38	96 60
27 59	15 58	19 68	95 47	25 69	11 90	26 19	07 40	83 59	90 95
95 98	45 52	27 35	86 81	16 29	37 60	39 35	05 24	49 00	29 07
12 95	72 72	81 84	36 58	05 10	70 50	31 04	12 67	74 01	72 90
35 23	06 68	52 50	39 55	92 28	28 89	64 87	80 00	84 53	97 97
86 33	95 73	80 92	26 49	54 50	41 21	06 62	73 91	35 05	21 37
02 82	96 23	16 46	15 51	60 31	55 27	84 14	71 58	94 71	48 35
44 46	34 96	32 68	48 22	40 17	43 25	33 31	26 26	59 34	99 00
08 77	07 19	94 46	17 51	03 73	99 89	28 44	16 87	56 16	56 09
61 59	37 08	08 46	56 76	29 48	33 87	70 79	03 80	96 81	79 68
67 70	18 01	67 19	29 49	58 67	08 56	27 24	20 70	46 31	04 32
23 09	08 79	18 78	00 32	86 74	78 55	55 72	58 54	76 07	53 73
89 40	26 39	74 58	59 55	87 11	74 06	49 46	31 94	86 66	66 97
84 95	66 42	90 74	13 71	00 71	24 41	67 62	38 92	39 26	30 29
52 14	49 02	19 31	28 15	51 01	19 09	97 94	52 43	22 21	17 66
89 56	31 41	37 87	28 16	62 48	01 84	46 06	04 39	94 10	76 21
65 94	05 93	06 68	34 72	73 17	65 34	00 65	75 78	23 97	13 04
13 08	15 75	02 83	48 26	53 77	62 96	56 52	28 26	12 15	75 53
03 18	33 57	16 71	60 27	15 18	39 32	37 01	05 86	25 14	35 41
10 04	00 95	85 04	32 80	19 01	85 03	29 29	80 04	21 52	14 76
23 94	97 28	60 43	42 25	26 48	48 13	34 68	39 22	74 85	03 25
35 63	42 90	90 74	33 17	58 77	83 36	76 22	00 89	61 55	13 17
42 86	03 36	45 33	60 77	72 92	10 76	22 55	11 00	37 60	47 73
67 26	92 87	09 96	85 37	82 61	39 01	70 05	12 66	17 39	99 34
91 93	88 56	35 76	97 35	19 37	14 66	07 57	24 41	06 90	07 72
37 14	73 35	32 01	07 94	78 28	90 33	71 56	63 77	89 24	24 28
07 46	50 58	08 73	42 97	20 42	64 68	48 35	04 38	28 28	36 94
92 18	09 46	94 99	17 41	28 60	67 94	26 54	63 70	84 73	76 61
00 49	98 43	39 67	68 40	41 31	92 28	49 57	15 55	11 81	41 89
08 59	41 41	33 59	43 28	14 51	02 71	24 45	41 57	22 11	79 79
67 05	19 54	32 33	34 68	27 93	39 35	62 51	35 55	40 99	46 19
24 99	48 06	96 41	21 25	29 03	57 71	96 49	94 74	98 90	21 52
65 86	27 46	70 93	27 39	64 37	01 63	21 03	43 78	18 74	77 07
52 70	03 20	84 96	14 37	51 05	63 99	81 02	84 56	17 78	48 45
32 88	29 93	58 21	71 05	68 58	79 08	86 37	98 76	70 45	66 23
54 16	39 40	98 57	02 05	65 15	73 23	51 51	75 06	38 13	51 68
95 22	18 59	54 57	44 22	72 35	81 24	14 94	24 04	42 26	92 14
93 10	27 94	90 45	39 33	50 26	88 46	90 57	40 47	71 63	62 59
19 20	85 20	15 67	78 03	32 23	50 59	24 83	64 99	18 00	78 50

Each digit is an independent sample from a population in which the digits 0 to 9 are equally likely, that is each has a probability of $\frac{1}{10}$.

Form No. 2.

Register No. 4913 Div. B Ward. 1 Cell. 12

Transferred to

DATE

16 July } 34

1872

RECEIVING BOOK.

Prisoner's Name. — James Dewley C. of E.

Last Residence. — Plough

Trade or Occupation. — Servant

Age.	Height.	Complexion.	Colour of Hair.	Colour of Eyes.	Visage.	Marks, &c.
15	5. 4	Fair	Brn	Brn	Oval	Moles on neck & on arms.

Apparent State of Health. — Good

Is he Lame or Ruptured? — No

Has he any Infectious Disease? — No

Caps.	Coats.	Smockfrocks.	Jackets.	Waistcoats.	Trowsers.	Breeches.	Drawers.	Gaiters.	Stockings.	Shoes.	Boots.	Shirts.	Flannel Shirts.	Handkerchiefs.	...	...	...	...	Tobacco Box.	Pocket Books.	...	...
1			1	1				1	1		1		1									

Observations on the state of Prisoner's Apparel, as to Cleanliness and Decency. — Clean

Place of Nativity. — Upton cum Chalvey

Father's { Name, — Wm Dewley

{ Trade, — Gardener

{ Residence, — Upton Park

Is Prisoner single, married, widow, or a widower? — Single

Wife or Husband's Residence.

Number of Children.

Age of { Eldest

{ Youngest

Degree of Instruction. — Imp

Forgery

Committed.

Magistrate's Name.

Warrant.

Trial at Assizes or Sessions, how disposed of. — Indicted Summer Assizes 1872

Convicted Summer Assizes 1872

3 Months H L

Discharged. — 15 October 1872

Evidence brought. — Rendered in Court

Has Prisoner been in the Army or Navy? If so, in what Regiment or Ship? — No

Conduct in Gaol. — Good

Has Prisoner been in Custody before? If so, when, and for what offence? — No

Contents   Unit 3

Objectives

After studying this unit you should be able to:

1 Recognize examples of implicit quantification.

2 Define nominal, ordinal and interval data and from Drake, 1973, give an example of each.

3 Define the terms *mode* and *median* and, given specific sets of data and specific problems, determine whether to use the *mean*, the *mode* or the *median* or more than one measure.

4 Identify bimodal, unimodal, symmetrical and negatively and positively skewed polygons.

5 Given a set of data produce a *histogram* and a *frequency polygon* from it.

6 Define the *range* of a distribution.

7 Given a set of data calculate its *standard deviation*.

8 Given appropriate data, estimate from a sample the mean of some population parameter at the ninety-five per cent confidence level.

9 Given appropriate data estimate from a sample the proportion of items in a population with a given attribute.

Describing data

1 Implicit and explicit quantification

I began the last unit by commenting on the everyday nature of sampling. I'm going to begin this one by pointing out that we use a great many numerical expressions in normal speech. Often these expressions are explicitly quantitative, that is to say they are couched in a numerical form. Very frequently, however, these numerical expressions appear in a verbal form.

To demonstrate what these are and how frequently they appear, as well as to provide some material for later exercises, I've drawn a sample of lines from my colleague, Professor Arthur Marwick's book, *The Deluge: British Society and the First World War*, Harmondsworth, Penguin 1967. Why this book? It happened I was reading it just at the time when I was thinking about this unit. As I read I noticed a number of verbal expressions that were implicitly quantitative. But, as I pointed out in Unit 2, such impressionistic evidence is treacherous. Only a count of such expressions would give me a reliable indication of the extent of their use. The only feasible way of doing this would be to take a sample. I chose to draw a systematic sample. As we discovered in Unit 2, a systematic sample takes much less time than a random one. And in this case there is no reason to believe that the feature we are seeking is likely to be distributed on each page in any regular manner. So by taking the first line of every other page, excluding bibliographies and references, we should end up with a representative sample of 156 lines from the 12,500 in the book. The lines that emerged from the sampling exercise appear below:

Two years ago I published a small book called *The Explosion of*
European society, including Britain, then this must certainly
Lived Then; to Jonathan Cape Ltd for excerpts from Robert
Geography is an important influence on history. Britain, an
'hearts. This deplorable neglect of science is sadly handicapping us'
-tered in what was officially termed the Greater London area $7\frac{1}{4}$
certain are people of the existence of this separate working
Elijah Sandham, whose only political outlet was in the local
1.2 supplementary earners, would spend about 25s.), including
It was not, however, the issues of social reform which dis-
'when men were more needed to speak and act up to their faith.'
and an atmosphere of panic and untempered emergency. The
announced that an ultimatum expiring at 11 p.m. (midnight in
These conversions, we shall discover, were not achieved
of the war. On 6 August Parliament authorized an increase in
'in a like manner as if such persons were subject to military law and'
'with snow on their boots' were passing through Britain on
advisory function only.[71] Executive power stayed in the
war. Allowances and pensions for the dependants of men on
spectacle of British planes in hot pursuit of the raider.[85] After
pure and simple'.[92] He now argues with great cogency that
'The effect of this revelation of the German mind on ourselves is'
stone were handing out white feathers to young men still to
inciting them to send their menfolk to the trenches. Among
which could be worn by men on vital production and thus
authority to sign the first agreement, a further special agree-
'of efficiency with respect to the due observance of the rules of the'
the new recruiting drive which was, in the end, to culminate in
flowed immediately, so that even the ranks of the brewing
But the Government had secured its verdict. The Defence
supplies as to combat drunkenness.[29] Scarcity conditions
creation of one vast industrial union which would be a centre
1915, when the three-year agreement then in force was due to
of War Act. The Government appointed a two-man Com-
-side. Just as the engineers on Clydeside had had a three-year

of the family unit; the suspicion that the main intention was
resign in order to be free to support it; the T.U.C. had just
to hear appeals based on 'a conscientious objection to the
on their hands, gave him a conditional – that is, conditional
itself.[72] For all that the individual workman might still feel
now outshone everyone in their patriotic fervour and stirring
desire to serve. This was more than could be borne by the
George Ministry had had six months to bear fruit, the figure
women's para-military organizations had sprung up, consoli-
The middle-class society at the end of the century, however,
woman question. In demonstrating their talents, women also
the men at the front know of the courage and discipline of
-selves; moreover, there was a strong current of feeling that,
to maintain their qualification) and no intention of holding a
For the 'specified age' the report suggested thirty or thirty-
about 1880 of efficient methods of mechanical contraception.
estimate of increased promiscuity, but for the illumination it
wrapped the question of venereal diseases in a web of guilt and
to the Middle Ages, when public-houses were not only fre-
One by-product of the entry of women into factories and in-
unadulterated alcohol. At the same time the dim stirrings of a
fourteen were governed by laws similar to, but more stringent
Youth, being central to every discussion of post-war de-
Surveying society as a whole in 1915 and 1916, Govern-
1916 there was a very sharp decline in the incidence of pau-
and demonstrations against the high cost of living, including
'Food, laundry, cleaning, etc. £130'
A journalist's description of the first Easter of the war shows
in his awareness that the cinema could be exploited for propa-
On the evidence of letters to the press and of the continued
censorship). 'There are some things better left undescribed.
into Waterloo after nightfall might find that their train sud-
the requirements of the twentieth-century constitution, show
audience including children, and 'A' certificates to those suit-
the upper-class life with which she was familiar, a great craze
his English Opera, which performed extensively in the pro-
specifically for them. At a time when much of the colour was
same writer continues, 'brought to rural Scotland a welcome
which, in effect, usually means State action, on behalf of the
All socialists, then, are collectivists (though some, for example
his castle and the poor man at his gate, it was part of the
United Kingdom, in practice about one fifth of the total mer-
had such abundant supplies that these commodities could, if
-ment, acting on the advice of a Committee on Chemicals
they were stuck with fistfuls of bad debts, while, at the same
for.' All such hints and proposals merely aroused the hearty
that experience of State control during the war has retarded
which called for the further step of control of profits.[37]
followed upon the utter disorganization of the first stages of
-trated on the National Register, the Derby Scheme, and con-
'produced at home. In regard to the milk industry, for instance, a'
solution must be combined the experience gained in both the
-mentary debate on food prices took place on 16 October.
-cessor. Asquith, in fact, was in greater degree an obstacle to the
also, his enemies said, more than a dash of his proclivity for
that the Unionists would not back him made him decide that
But the main reason turns us again towards the basic explana-
1917, in a war of ironic equivocation, was the most equivocal

Figure 1 Agreement between the master of a merchant ship and his crew, as to pay and conditions, 1847. Source: Public Record Office, BT 98/1173

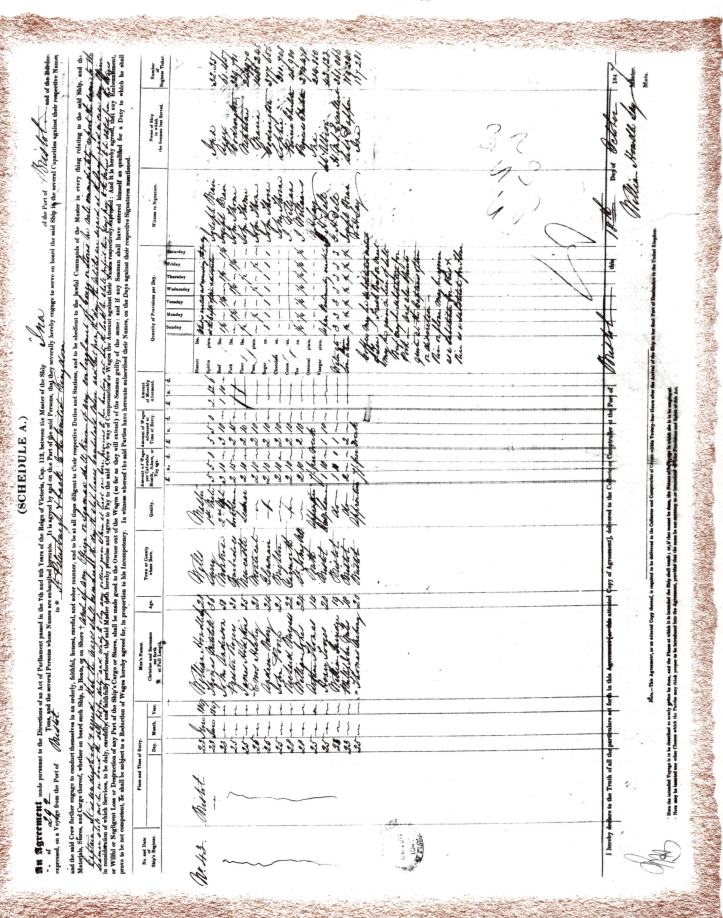

Figure 2 Page from the manuscript poll-book for the Parliamentary election of 1835, in Bath. Source: Guildhall, Bath

No.	NAMES.	Trade or Profession.	Residence.	PALMER.	ROEBUCK.	DAUBENEY.		
				74	75	97		
1214	Davis Edwd	Innkeeper	Wells Road	1				
1154	Drace Jos	Gent	Widcombe Hill			1		
1232	Fear Wm	Carpenter	Holloway		1			
1170	Paker Jas	Poultry Dealer	Holloway	1	1			
1195	Cottle Geo	Gent	Wells Road	1	1			
1255	Hunt Jno	Poulterer	Claverton Pl		1	1		
1203	Jackson Jas	Esq	Devonshire Pl		1			
1202	Cleaves Chas	Publican	Ebenezer Terr	1	1			
1356	Stenstone Jr	Schoolmaster	Widcombe Hill	1	1			
1353	Sherland Isaac	Taylor	Foxhill Pl			1		
1278	Haydon Jas Geo	Conveyancer	Oxford Terr			1		
1252	Grist Jas	Ferryman	Bristol Road	1	1		Close of first day Poll	
1198	Coulthart Jas	Teadealer	Wells Road	1	1			
1239	Lansdown Jos	Gent	Caroline Bdgs			1		
1177	Landy Jno	Farmer	Lyncombe	1	1			
1194	Crease Geo	Gardener	Wells Road			1		
1397	Wickham Jno	Grocer	Pulteney St		1			
1201	Collins Philip	Farmer	Oddadown	1	1			
1209	Denman Giles	Baker	Bristol Road	1	1			
1268	Howell Geo	Clerk	Bristol Road	1	1			
1286	King Michl	Coachman	Caroline Bdgs	1	1			
1229	Fisher Chas	Painter	River Park Pl			1		
1267	Hoar Francis	Draper	Caroline Bdgs	1	1			
1254	Hamper Chas	Draper	Lyncombe			1		
1103	Cruttwell Richd	Gent	Hangingland	1		1		
1409	Wood Geo	Shoemaker	Claverton St	1	1			
1307	Morris Thos	Mason	Sussex Pl		1			
1412	Weaver Geo	Shoemaker	Sussex Pl		1 1			
				89	93	47		

begun should end in a blaze of definitive glory to be achieved
typists, any temptation to attribute a magical quality of reform
cards in July 1917. Lord Rhondda's directive of August setting
Shortages and standardization of available foods contributed
town which suffered most of all was Dover, especially in the
'In order to utilize to the best advantage imported meat'
consolidated by the great patriotic prestige which business-
grievance, the attempts by private employers to extend dilu-
Housing was a background cause of the rising ire of the
a remedy they recommended a programme of social legisla-
Man Power Act which made a bonfire of most of the remain-
But beyond these relatively innocuous matters, propaganda
enterprise – that of *The Times*. For the Government Lord
Atrocities Committee, were known as the Bryce group; these
-tion which is glossed by the subheading inserted in the
one year was enough to turn enthusiasm sour: as F. H.
'So Abram rose, and clave the wood, and went,'
visionary scheme of a whole collection of war paintings, to
rather than towards the establishment of abstract relation-
From its labours there sprang the not very successful national
August 1913, it was really the war which got it off the ground;
flage was a French idea, taken up in this country by the Royal
munication Germany would have been completely cut off
added up to give a new scientific orientation to British society
More relevant to the main purpose is the manner in which
much a question of rebuilding society as it was before the
profession, and the insurance committees and approved
Fisher himself submitted a short, succinct report to the
universities.[51] In 1920 two hundred State Scholarships were
designed to bring down the price of bread to 9d. a quartern
European Allies, all of whom were by now largely dependent
with military contractors, but with the ordinary textile
a feeble and half-hearted fashion. There was, too, an obvious
The second Battle of the Marne of July 1918 was the first
was guest at the Lord Mayor's Banquet; although the more
'-ing a dinner-gong and a parson marching at the head of a group of'
integrate completely the anti-war and pro-war elements, to
exaggerated'.[20] One hundred and seven out of 707 seats were
Lloyd George to proceed with his reconstruction plans for a
who would be released in the order of importance of their
The new year opened with the publication of the Govern-
-tinued: for meat till November 1919, for butter till early 1920,
of the established order: Willie Gallacher and Emanuel Shin-
in these new houses. The existing controlled rents of working-
Reconstruction and the Bad Fairy Bolshevism, the purchase
would not be strong enough to secure the prolongation or
Controller, while unsure about nationalization, favoured
permanently stilled; correspondingly the fears aroused among
we've got'. Within the Conservative Party Lord Robert
forth all sorts of different responses from all sorts of different
figure, it virtually ceased to exist as the sort of social demarca-
and opinion-makers began to stress his claim upon a fuller
form in which it actually came, was a consequence of the
portion to moral or material gains made, to foster scepticism,
Geography, naturally, did not change much between 1914
was concerned in the years before 1914, but greatly extended
exaggerated because the classification in 1921 was rather more
in primary poverty, the new wage rates should have reduced

character' the attempt should also be made to 'lift' the public
'object aimed at is not to instruct or "uplift", but to amuse, and in'
sources of endless self-congratulation on the part of the War
socialistic theory had vindicated itself during the war, and
presented, not argued over. Its greatest significance is as a

Reading through the above 156 lines is not an easy task. Professor Marwick will never forgive me for presenting his very readable work in this way! However, if you have gone through them you may have noticed the lines do contain examples of both *implicit* and *explicit* measurement. On my count 38 lines contained instances of the latter. All but one of these expressions were unequivocally precise (ie two, $7\frac{1}{4}$, 1.2, 25, 11, midnight, etc.). The one exception was 'Middle Ages', about the dating of which there is some dispute. My point in drawing your attention to these lines, is however, not so much to note the examples of explicit quantification, but to alert you to the implicit measures. These are, in fact, far more numerous. In the first half of the list (78 lines) I noted the following:

The figure 38 as a proportion of all the lines in the sample is $38 \div 156 = 0.24$ or just short of $\frac{1}{4}$; or in percentage terms, $\frac{38}{156} \times 100 = 24.4\%$. From our work in Unit 2 we know this *sample statistic* bears some relation to the corresponding *population parameter*. We know it is more or less ($\pm$ in arithmetical terms) close to that figure. Later in this unit we shall show how we can calculate just how close it is.

small; certainly; excerpts; important; sadly; certain; separate; Greater; more; local; only; untempered; increase; a like manner; hot pursuit; great; vital; in the end; ranks; scarcity; vast; centre; main; more; middle-class; strong current; increased; same; similar; more stringent; central; as a whole; very sharp; incidence; high; upper-class; familiar; great; extensively; specifically; much; in effect; usually; poor; all; some; part; abundant.

SAQ 1 Make a list of the examples of implicit quantification in the last 78 lines from Professor Marwick's work cited above. Answer at the end of the unit.

The first point to make about these examples of implicit quantification is that their number is by no means negligible. If 78 lines contain 48 examples then the book as a whole, with its approximately 12,480 lines (312 pages of text $\times$ 40 lines per page) could contain $\dfrac{12,480}{78} \times 48 = 7,680$ such expressions. A second point is that implicit quantification does limit one's understanding of whatever is being described. Whether the matter under discussion is intrinsically important or not is irrelevant. That is a value judgement which will vary from individual to individual and situation to situation. To illustrate this, let's take the first three examples listed above; 'small', 'certainly', 'excerpts'. The first of these refers to the size of Professor Marwick's book, *The Explosion of British Society, 1914–62*. One must presume the 'small' refers to the number of pages rather than the shape of the book and is not due to extreme modesty on Professor Marwick's part. If my presumption is correct, would you think it unfair of me to set the following as a self-assessment question, let alone a computer-marked assignment? I would!

SAQ 2 Professor Marwick describes his book, *The Explosion of British Society, 1914–62*, as 'small'. How many pages does 'small' represent? From the list below select the correct one.
108 pages
158 pages
208 pages
258 pages

The second expression, 'certainly', like the words 'important', 'relevant', 'significant', is open to various interpretations. It comes in the sentence – 'If we accept, as we must, that the war was partly the result of forces and tensions developing in early twentieth-century European society, including Britain, then this must certainly serve as a qualification upon any attempt to analyse the consequences of the war for British society' (pp 8–9). The use of 'certainly' here implies the rejection of such alternative hypotheses as, for example, that which would emerge if the word 'not' were placed after 'certainly' or if the word 'might' were placed before it. Also, though 'certainly' normally means 'without doubt' in the context of this sentence, associated, as it is, with the word 'qualification', the strength of the certainty is not made explicit. Does it suggest to you that the 'qualification' in question is the most important one to be considered; one of equivalent status to many others or, indeed, one that is to be noted but, relatively speaking, is of minor significance?

The third expression of implicit quantification was 'excerpts'. This refers to quotations from other works appearing in the book. Quite obviously in this context, there would be little point in putting anything more precise than this. On the other hand in preparing this unit it would be no good me sending a note to the Open University copyrights department stating that I wished to use 'excerpts' from Professor Marwick's book *The Explosion of British Society, 1914–62*: the reason, of course, being that for quotations totalling more than 400 words, permission has to be sought from the author and publisher.

It has been argued that implicit measurement is 'usually . . . crude, uncontrolled and subject to serious misunderstanding and error.' (Dollar and Jensen p 8.) You must judge whether the examples just discussed, or those in the whole sample, deserve such strictures. Certainly they are not, to adopt West's phrase, 'the most arresting and colourful instances' (Drake 1973 p 110). But to have argued from such instances would have been to negate one of the most important lessons of Unit 2.

SAQ 3   What is this lesson?

This discussion of implicit and explicit quantification is intended as a prelude to our examination of certain explicit measures. Before tackling this, however, please read Floud 1973 pp 8–15, where you will find the different ways in which one can classify data. The next section of this unit assumes that you have grasped the difference between *nominal, ordinal* and *interval* data.

SAQ 4   The cover of this unit gives various kinds of data about a prisoner who spent some time in Aylesbury Jail in 1872. Classify the data according to whether it is nominal, ordinal or interval.

2 Measures of central tendency

As an introduction to this section we will reiterate two points made earlier. First, in seeking to aid the development of general laws of human behaviour we may need to analyse large amounts of data. Second, to facilitate this task we may use the technique of sampling. Even, then, however, we may find ourselves wishing to abridge our data still further, to encapsulate in one or two figures its principal characteristics. In this section of the unit we shall be examining ways of doing this by locating the centre of a *frequency* distribution: in the next we shall be examining ways of measuring how a distribution is dispersed around its centre.

We'll begin by looking again at the *Bath Poll Book* for 1855. Let's focus our attention on the first thirty votes recorded for Whateley which happen to be the total set of those of his voters whose names began with the letter 'A'. The poll book gives the occupation of each of these voters. This is nominal data. A quick glance down the list shows that several voters had the same occupation. One way of summarizing the data then would be to group the voters by occupation as in Table 1. In drawing up this list I merely went through the names as they appeared in the poll book. I could have put them in a different order, say according to the frequency with which each occurred, heading the list with the biggest and finishing with the smallest. In our case this wouldn't involve much re-arrangement as so many of our occupations occurred only once. In fact all we would need to do would be to put 'Lodging House Keeper' after, or possibly before, 'Clergyman'. Alternatively I could have listed the occupations in alphabetical order. But whatever I did, my listing would have been arbitrary. There is no natural order. It is, therefore, a bit difficult to talk about the *centre* of this particular distribution. However, you will note that there is a quite

478

NAME— *Judge D'Arcy*

Date of Birth... ... *31 July 1867*

Name and Profession of Father ... ... } *August 3 d'Arcy Rosslan, Mindanao Ballynavoing*

Place of Birth ... *Iromgetown Coltanney*

Date and Place of Marriage ... }

Special Attainments or Qualifications.

Dates of Orders and Commissions.

Rewards and Distinctions.

Examinations.

SHIP.	Station.	Date of Appointment.	Date of Discharge.	Cause.	Date of Report.	General Conduct.	Ability.	Zeal.	Judgment.	Temper.	Professional Knowledge.	If Temperate.	Physical Qualities.	Performance of Special Duties.	If deserving of advancement.	REMARKS.

Table 1 Occupations of the 30 Whateley
voters whose surnames begin with the
letter 'A'

Occupation	Number
Gentleman	10
Clergyman	2
Confectioner	1
Florist	1
Shirtmaker	1
Builder	1
Captain	1
Gardener	1
Tailor	1
Lodging House Keeper	2
Pawnbroker	1
Sexton	1
Cabinet Maker	1
Wine Merchant	1
Baker	1
Livery Stable Keeper	1
Draper's Assistant	1
Grocer	1
General	1
Total	30

definite clustering of occupations. The number of 'gentlemen' far outstrips any other. This occupation occurs most *frequently*. The statistician's term for the most frequently occurring observation is the *mode*. Graphically it can be represented as in the bar chart in Figure 4. Here the height of the columns, or bars, represents the numbers

Figure 4 Bar chart showing occupations of thirty Whateley voters whose surnames begin with the letter A.

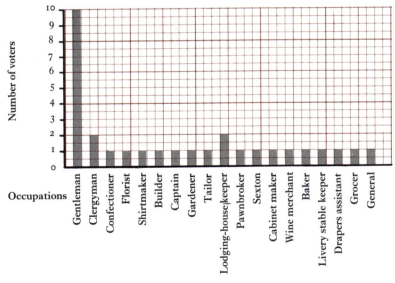

in each occupation, that is the frequency with which they occur. This particular distribution (of occupations) is called *unimodal* because *one* occupation is bigger than any other. If there had been no gentlemen in our list, but otherwise the distribution of occupations had been the same, then two occupations would have been of equal size (Clergyman and Lodging House Keeper) and each would have exceeded all the other occupations in size. Such a distribution would be called *bimodal*.

SAQ 5   Draw a bar chart, on the lines of Figure 4, to show the distribution of those of Whateley's voters whose names begin with the letter 'O'. Is the distribution unimodal or bimodal?

The mode is a useful summary of the kind of distribution shown in Figure 4. It is not, of course, particularly useful if there is little clustering in the data. The mode is the only measure we can use on nominal data. If, however, we have ordinal data we can use not only the mode, but also another measure, the *median*. The mode, we have seen, is the most frequently occurring observation in a set of observations: the median is the middle value in a set of observations. To be able to find the middle, the observations must be ordered in one way or another. Let us look again at the voters in Table 1 above. We could, if we wished, impose some sort of order on the list, by allocating each occupation to a social class. We'll do this using Armstrong's classification system (Wrigley 1972 pp 215–23). We see from Table 2 that the thirty voters are by no

Table 2 Social classification of the 30 Whateley voters whose surnames begin with the letter 'A'.

Class		Number
I	Gentleman (10); Clergyman (2); Captain (1); General (1)	14
II	—	—
III	Confectioner (1); Florist (1); Shirtmaker (1); Builder (1); Tailor (1); Lodging House Keeper (2); Pawnbroker (1); Sexton (1); Cabinet Maker (1); Wine Merchant (1); Baker (1); Livery Stable Keeper (1); Draper's Assistant (1); Grocer (1)	15
IV	Gardener (1)	1
V	—	—
	Total	30

means evenly distributed across the five classes. The median occupation lies in Class III. Notice, however, it could very easily have fallen in Class I had the latter had another couple of voters in it. The table, in fact, suggests a not uninteresting division between the voters. But more of this when we come to the units on historical psephology.

SAQ 6   Which is the modal class of the distribution in Table 2?

So far we have seen that the mode can be used to locate the central tendency of a distribution of nominal data and that both the mode and the median can be used for the same purpose when we have ordinal data. With interval data we have a choice of three measures, for to the mode and the median we can add the arithmetic *mean*. This latter measure is widely known. In common parlance it is what we usually speak of as the 'average'. For statisticians the mode and the median are also averages. Since we have already used the mean in Unit 2, we will not linger over it here. Drawing on our 'A' voters again, let us calculate the mean rateable value of the property which provided the first thirty in the list of Whateley's voters with their franchise. Table 3 shows the values. As we've said already, with interval data one has a choice of using the mode, the median or the mean to measure the central tendency of a distribution. This facility, of course, brings the problems of choice

Table 3 Rateable values of property enfranchising the 30 Whateley voters whose surnames begin with the letter 'A'

£	£	£	£	£	£
45	75	100	16	50	65
28	18	70	75	28	22
55	110	47	50	45	90
60	20	18	140	43	50
30	60	11	40	55	60
218 +	283 +	246 +	321 +	221 +	287 = 1576

$$\text{Mean} = \frac{1576}{30} = £52\frac{1}{2}$$

This is one used by Dr. W. A. Armstrong in his study of the York of 1851. Anyone considering a project on social stratification in this period using census enumerators' returns should read his contributions to E. A. Wrigley (ed), 1972, *Nineteenth-Century Society : Essays in the Use of Quantitative Methods for the Study of Social Data,* Cambridge, Cambridge University Press pp 191-310. For a discussion of the use of occupations for the purposes of social classification see the articles by Thernstrom and Blumin in Drake 1973 pp 221-49.

with it. Which, in any particular instance, is the most appropriate measure? This depends partly on what we want to show and partly on the shape of the distribution.

SAQ 7   What are the modal and median values of this distribution?

Figure 5 Bar chart showing frequency distribution of the rateable values of property enfranchising the thirty Whateley voters whose surnames begin with the letter 'A'.

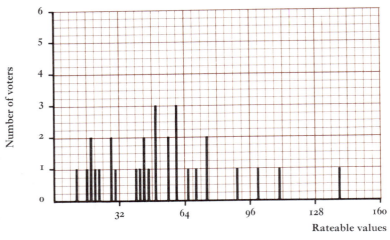

Figure 5 shows, in the form of a bar chart, the distribution of the rateable values of the first thirty voters listed for Whateley. They range from £11 to £140, but there is a considerable clustering around the £16–£30 mark and again from £40–£60. We can bring out this feature a little more clearly if, instead of plotting each individual value, we put them into groups, say from £10–£19; £20–£29; £30–£39 and so on up to £140–£149. We can plot our efforts in the form of a *histogram* as in Figure 6.

Figure 6 Histogram showing the distribution of the rateable values of property enfranchising the thirty Whateley voters whose surnames begin with the letter 'A', grouped in classes with £10 intervals.

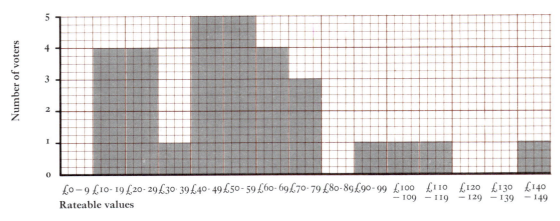

To summarize our distribution, visually at least, even further, we can take two more steps. First, we can produce a *frequency polygon* by drawing a line connecting the mid-points of each of the £10 classes. This we have done in Figure 7, which reveals even more clearly than our histogram, the basic structure of our distribution. Our final step is to produce a visual representation which goes as far as is possible, short of using mathematical methods, to produce the essence of the distribution. We draw a smooth line whose course best fits the trend revealed by the frequency polygon. The result appears in Figure 8.

Figure 7 Frequency polygon of the data in Figure 5

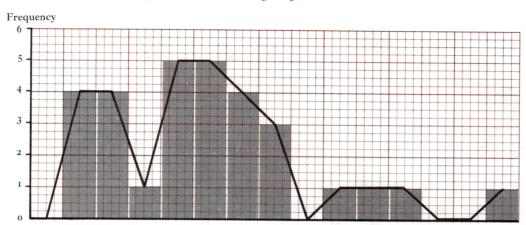

Going back to our original data, presented in Table 3 and Figure 5, we see that the distribution is bimodal (three voters have rateable values of £50 and three have ones of £60); the mean is £52.5 and the median is £50. The fact that the three measures of central tendency are relatively close suggests a symmetrical distribution. *The* characteristic of a perfectly symmetrical distribution, or 'normal curve', is that the mean, mode and median have the same value. However, in the case of the Whateley voters, the symmetry is something of a delusion. What appears to have happened, and Figure 8 shows this clearly, is that a relatively large number of small values to the left of the modal interval have been balanced by a few, high values, to the right. Our example, then, shows how careful one must be in using the three measures of central tendency. Distributions can take a variety of shapes and sometimes it is necessary to show the mode, median and mean if one is to avoid giving a misleading impression. For a good illustration of this, see Floud 1973 pp 82–4.

In describing frequency distributions we have, so far, examined only measures of *central tendency*. Handled with care they can tell us, in a very succinct manner, some of the key features of such distributions. But even in the most favourable circumstances they tell us only part of what we often want to know. Let me explain by means of an illustration. It may bring back memories of the distribution of sample means we drew for the Whateley and Tite voters in Unit 2. Before proceeding then, have a look at SAQ 8.

Figure 8 Curve, fitted by eye, showing the distribution in Figure 7

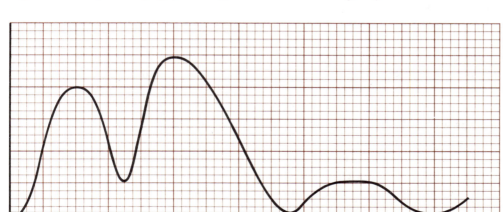

SAQ 8 Here are two distributions of voters according to their rateable values.

Voter's Rateable Values (£s)

CANDIDATE A: 40, 60, 10, 50, 30, 30, 20, 70, 50, 20, 30, 40, 60, 40, 40, 50

CANDIDATE B: 20, 40, 30, 50, 60, 50, 50, 40, 30, 40, 40, 30, 30, 50, 40, 40

Using the graph paper below plot in the form of a histogram the distribution of votes by rateable values for the two candidates.

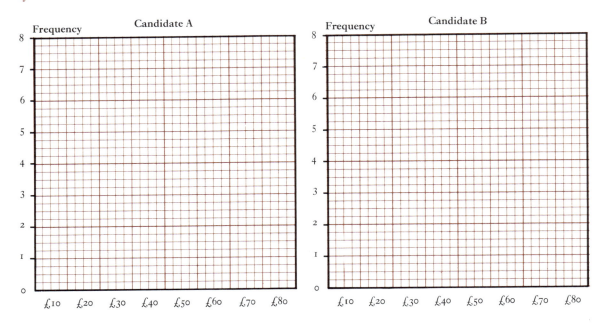

Calculate for each candidate the mode, median and mean voter's rateable value.

It will be obvious from your answer to SAQ 8 (assuming you got it right!) that the two distributions differ in one, possibly important regard. Despite the fact that they both have the same median, mode, and mean (they are both normal 'curves'), the distribution of Candidate A's voters is more spread out, more *dispersed*, than that of Candidate B's. Our measures of central tendency appear to have given us only half the story; to get the whole we need to calculate the extent to which our distributions are dispersed.

3 Measures of dispersion

The most obvious measure of dispersion and the easiest to calculate is the *range*. We have already used this, without making any mention of the fact, because it is so obvious, being the difference between the highest and lowest values in the distribution. Looking back at the exercises we did in Unit 2 with the first eight recorded votes for Whateley and Tite, we see that for the former the range was from £20–£110; for the latter £10–£40. In this case the range does tell us something; it does help us to distinguish between the two distributions. To take another example look at the distributions in SAQ 8 in Unit 2. That for candidate A was from £10–£70; that for B was narrower, being from £20–£60. Again the range is useful. But suppose in any of these distributions we had had an *outlier*, that is to say, a value that lay a long way from the bulk of the observations in the distribution. In a large sample, or population, such an outlier would make little difference to the median and the mode. It might have more effect on the mean. Its effect on the range would, however, probably be such as to render it useless as a generalization about the dispersion of the distribution.

SAQ 9 Can you justify the comments I have just made about the mode, median, mean and range?

What we need, then, is a measure of dispersion which takes into account *all* the values of the distribution and not just the two extreme ones. The measure most commonly used to fulfil this purpose is the *standard deviation*. The calculation of this measure is easy, but tedious. To make it as straightforward as possible, turn to the set of instructions below this headed – *A Guide to Calculation: the standard deviation*. You will see that the Guide is divided into three columns. In the first column (the left-hand one) is the calculation in symbols; in the second we have turned this into words and in the third we have worked out an example. We will now go through this stage by stage.

First of all we re-write the standard deviation formula to eliminate the need to calculate the mean rateable value.[1]

> The standard deviation tells us to what extent the values of the distribution are – or are not – bunched around the mean. The formula for calculating it – $\sqrt{\dfrac{\Sigma\,(X - \bar{X})^2}{N}}$ takes into account the amount by which each value deviates from the mean (that is, in the $X - \bar{X}$ part of the formula), which is what makes it so much more useful in most cases than the range.

A Guide to Calculation: the standard deviation

In symbols	In words	Examples
$S = \sqrt{\dfrac{\Sigma(X - \bar{X})^2}{N}}$ $= \sqrt{\dfrac{N\Sigma X^2 - (\Sigma X)^2}{N}}$	The standard deviation for	Rateable value of property held by eight Tite voters William Abraham £40 Henry Adams £20 Thomas Adams £20 Hilar Aicher £20 Charles Ainsworth £30 James Aldous £40 Charles Allen £10 Francis Thomas Allen £20
X^2	A Square each of the observations of rateable value of property held by Tite voters. That is, multiply each number by itself	$40 \times 40 = 1600$ $20 \times 20 = 400$ $20 \times 20 = 400$ $20 \times 20 = 400$ $30 \times 30 = 900$ $40 \times 40 = 1600$ $10 \times 10 = 100$ $20 \times 20 = 400$
ΣX^2	B Add up, or sum, the squared values resulting from Stage A. Σ is the Greek letter *sigma*, meaning 'the sum of . . .'	ΣX^2 $1600 + 400 + 400 + 400 + 900 + 1600 + 100 + 400 = 5800$
$N\Sigma X^2$	C Multiply the number resulting from Stage B by the total number of observations. The symbol used for this is 'N'. As we are looking at the rateable values of eight voters, our $N = 8$.	$N\Sigma X^2$ $8 \times 5800 = 46400$
ΣX	D Sum the eight observations	ΣX $40 + 20 + 20 + 20 + 30 + 40 + 10 + 20 = 200$
$(\Sigma X)^2$	E Square the number resulting from Stage D	$(\Sigma X)^2$ $(200)^2 = 200 \times 200 = 40000$
$N\Sigma X^2 - (\Sigma X)^2$	F We now subtract the number obtained in Stage E ($(\Sigma X)^2 = 40000$) from the number obtained at Stage C ($N\Sigma X^2 = 46400$)	$N\Sigma X^2 - (\Sigma X)^2$ $46400 - 40000$ $= 6400$
$\sqrt{N\Sigma X^2 - (\Sigma X)^2}$	G Take the square root of the number resulting from Stage F	$\sqrt{6400} = 80$
$\sqrt{\dfrac{N\Sigma X^2 - (\Sigma X)^2}{N}}$	H Finally divide the result of Stage G by the number of observations (N)	$\dfrac{80}{8} = 10$

1 In fact this is not strictly necessary when calculating the standard deviation for such a small distribution as the one in our example – only eight observations.

In practice, however, this is a variation of the formula more commonly used by statisticians because it makes the calculation easier when working with large numbers of observations. For that reason we have used it for our examples here.

This rewriting is done by a mathematical manipulation of the original formula, the details of which need not concern us here. We can now go on to the actual calculation.

Stage A in Guide From the formula we see that the first thing we need to know is the value of each X^2, that is, the square of each of our eight observations. The symbol X is always used to denote the values we are working on.

Stage B Here we simply add up all our X^2s, making 5,800.

Stage C To complete the calculation of the first part of the formula – $N\Sigma X^2$ – we need to multiply the total of our X^2s arrived at in Stage B by the number of observations, N. This gives us a value of 46,400 ($8 \times 5,800$).

Stage D We now move on to the next part of the formula – $(\Sigma X)^2$ – and add up, first of all, the eight observations, ΣX, which make 200.

Stage E As we want $(\Sigma X)^2$, we square the sum of our eight observations, or multiply 200×200.

Stage F We have completed the calculation of the second part of the formula, and we now have to subtract that result from the result of the first part, arrived at in Stage C; that is, we subtract $(\Sigma X)^2$, which is 40,000 from $N\Sigma X^2$, which is 46,400, to get 6,400.

Stage G We see from the formula that the next step is to take the square root of 6,400.

Stage H Finally, the result of all foregoing calculations – 80 – is divided by the number of observations, N, which is 8, to give us our standard deviation of 10.

There is no need to memorize this standard deviation formula now. By the time you have finished SAQ 10, you should be familiar enough with it!

SAQ 10 Find the standard deviation of
a the distribution of Whateley's eight voters, given on the answer to SAQ 1 of Unit 2;
b the distribution of the rateable values of the voters for Candidate A, given in SAQ 8 for Unit 3;
c ditto for the voters for Candidate B.

Your answers to SAQ 10 will have demonstrated that the standard deviation is a useful way of summarizing the extent of dispersion around the mean in any particular distribution. You will notice that your answers to SAQ 10 (*a*) and 10 (*b*) are particularly interesting in this regard, because these two distributions had the same mean, mode and median. So, without the standard deviation, we might have been led to believe the distributions were more similar than was in fact the case. The standard deviation is then an important summary measure in its own right. Its value, however, is enhanced by being used in other statistical situations, to one of which, sampling, we will now return.

4 A return to sampling

You may remember that in Unit 2 we did a lot of rather tedious arithmetic to show that by calculating the mean value of samples of different sizes we were able to say how confident we were that the mean of any particular sample would lie more or less (in literary terms: $\pm$ in statistical ones) near the mean of the population.

In our examples we knew the particular *population parameter* (the mean), so that we could prove that our *sample statistic* was within a particular interval around the population mean. We could demonstrate quite definitely that, for example, in the case of Tite's eight voters, with a sample size of 4, then in sixty-two out of seventy samples, the sample mean was somewhere between £20 and £30 (see Unit 2 Table 6). But what if we had not known what the mean of the population was? Then obviously we would not have known how near our sample mean was to it. And, of course, usually we do not know what the population mean is (or any other parameter for that matter) since that is an objective of our sampling. It is here that the *standard deviation* comes to our rescue.

Turn back to Figure 12 of Unit 2. After looking at it for a moment turn to Figure 9 in this unit. Our figure in Unit 2 showed the results of an actual calculation in a particular situation. It was a graphical representation of a statement that with a sample of size 4, we know that the mean of eighty-nine per cent of our samples lay within ($\pm$) £5 of the population mean of £25. Our figure in this unit has *generalized*

Figure 9 Normal distribution curve

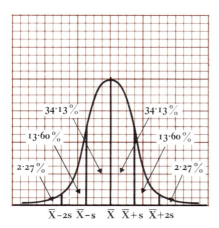

$$\overline{X}_{-2s} \quad \overline{X}_{-s} \quad \overline{X} \quad \overline{X}_{+s} \quad \overline{X}_{+2s}$$

that statement. It applies not to one particular set of samples but to all sets where we know the mean and standard deviation of the sample. It tells us that, given a random sample above a certain size (as Floud 1973 p 165 says 'in practice larger than 100'), then 68.26 per cent of all such random samples (34.13 per cent + 34.13 per cent) will have a mean that lies within an interval of *one* standard deviation above the population mean and *one* standard deviation below it. Furthermore it tells us that 95.46 per cent of all random samples (34.13 per cent + 34.13 per cent + 13.60 per cent + 13.60 per cent) will have a mean that lies within an interval of *two* standard deviations above the population mean, and *two* standard deviations below it.

We are now nearing the crux of the matter. How do we decide how close the mean of one of our random samples is to the population mean, when we do not know either the mean or the standard deviation of the population? The answer lies in a formula (to put it crudely) based on the relationships we have just been discussing. By using this formula we can find out the two things that we need to know. We want to estimate the population mean by using the mean of the particular random sample we have drawn; and we want to know how much reliance we can place on the estimate. As you would expect, the more precise we try to make the estimate, the less sure we can be that we are right, and vice versa. The first question can be restated in this form: we know the sample mean, and we know from our previous discussion that the sample mean is related to the population mean, so that we can estimate the percentage of sample means that will fall within a certain interval either side of the population mean. What is that interval, which we shall call the *confidence interval?* How big it is will be determined, in part, by how confident we want to be that the mean of our particular sample lies within it. Since we could have taken hundreds, perhaps thousands of samples, each one containing a different combination of items from the population, it is clear that as a result of *sampling error* some of them are going to be outside the interval. It follows that the wider the interval the fewer there will be outside and conversely the narrower the interval, the more there will be outside. So we are faced with a dilemma. If we want to be confident that virtually all the sample means we could possibly have calculated (say 95.46 per cent of them) will lie within the interval, then we will have to make that interval a big one (ie stretching from two standard deviations below the population mean to two above it). On the other hand, if we want a smaller interval, one that stretches no more than one standard deviation below the population mean and one above it, we must sacrifice certainty. For in this latter situation we can only be confident that about two in three of our sample means (68.26 per cent) will lie within this particular confidence interval. Our *confidence level*, as it is called, will then depend upon the size of *confidence interval* we want and vice versa. Thus the confidence interval enables us to estimate the population mean from the sample mean, and the confidence level tells us how much reliance we can place on our estimate. If this explanation is unclear go back to Table 6 and SAQ 4 in Unit 2 and try to tease out the position from them.

To demonstrate this technique let us go back to Unit 2 and our random sample of 200 Whateley voters. Let us assume that we don't know the mean rateable value of *all* Whateley voters, but want to estimate this from our sample. We will go through the steps necessary to produce this result, as we did when we calculated the standard deviation.

A Guide to Calculation: estimating the population mean from a sample

In symbols	In words	Example
$a = \bar{X} \pm \dfrac{2S}{(N-1)}$	The population mean	To find the mean rateable value of Whateley voters from a random sample of 200, at the 95.46% confidence level.
X	A Calculate the mean of the sample	Sum the 200 values ie £36 + £30 + £15 . . . . £52 + £12 + £82 = £9876. Divide by 200 = £49.4
S	B Calculate the standard deviation of the sample	See Guide to Calculation of standard deviation (£37.8) S = £37.8
$(N-1)$	C Subtract 1 from the number (N) of observations in the sample	$200 - 1 = 199$
$\sqrt{N-1}$	D Take the square root of $(N-1)$	$\sqrt{199} = 14.1$
$\dfrac{S}{\sqrt{N-1}}$	E Divide the standard deviation (S) by the square root of $(N-1)$	$\dfrac{37.8}{14.1} = 2.7$
$\dfrac{2S}{\sqrt{N-1}}$	F Multiply the sum reached at the end of *Stage E* by 2	$2.7 \times 2 = 5.4$
$\bar{X} \pm \dfrac{2S}{\sqrt{N-1}}$	At the 95% confidence level the population mean was 49.4 ± 5.4	

Stages A and B These are both straightforward repeats of earlier exercises.
Stage C The reason for this stage need not detain us. However, you will note that the bigger the sample size (N) the less important this stage will be, since the 1 we subtract will form a smaller and smaller proportion of N.
Stages D, E and F These three stages involve no new technique. We can now say that at the 95.46 per cent (usually abbreviated to 95 per cent) level of confidence the population mean will be £49.4 ± £5.4. Or, to put it another way, we can be confident that 95 per cent of random samples we draw of size 200 will have a mean value that lies in the *confidence interval* of £44–£54.8. Alternatively we can say that 68 per cent of such samples will lie in the confidence interval of £46.7–£52.1 or, put another way, £49.4 ± £2.7. This is an interval of *one* standard deviation either side of the mean.

SAQ 11 Estimate the mean rateable value of the property held by Tite's voters at the 95 per cent confidence level, using the data derived from the systematic sample of 236 voters given in the answer to SAQ 10 of Unit 2.

We will now do one final exercise. Suppose we wanted to find what proportion of items there were in a population with a particular attribute. For example, let us suppose we wanted to know what proportion of lines in Professor Marwick's book,

Figure 10 Photographs from Aylesbury Prison Register, 1872-73. Source: Bucks County Record Office, Aylesbury

Register number: 5432
Occupation: soldier
Age: 28
Marital status: single
Crime: stole a plaice
Sentence: 14 days hard labour

Register number: 5854
Occupation: laundress
Age: 59
Marital status: widow
Crime: stole shirts and jacket
Sentence: 1 month hard labour

Register number: 5293
Occupation: agricultural labourer
Age: 16
Marital status: single
Crime: obtained goods by false pretences
Sentence: 1 month hard labour

Register number: 5417
Occupation: domestic servant
Age: 19
Marital status: single
Crime: stole pair of gloves
Sentence: 14 days hard labour

Figure 11 Part of the 'preliminary statement' on Harlow Churchgate School, required for applications for government grants, 1873. Source: Public Record Office, ED 7/29/180

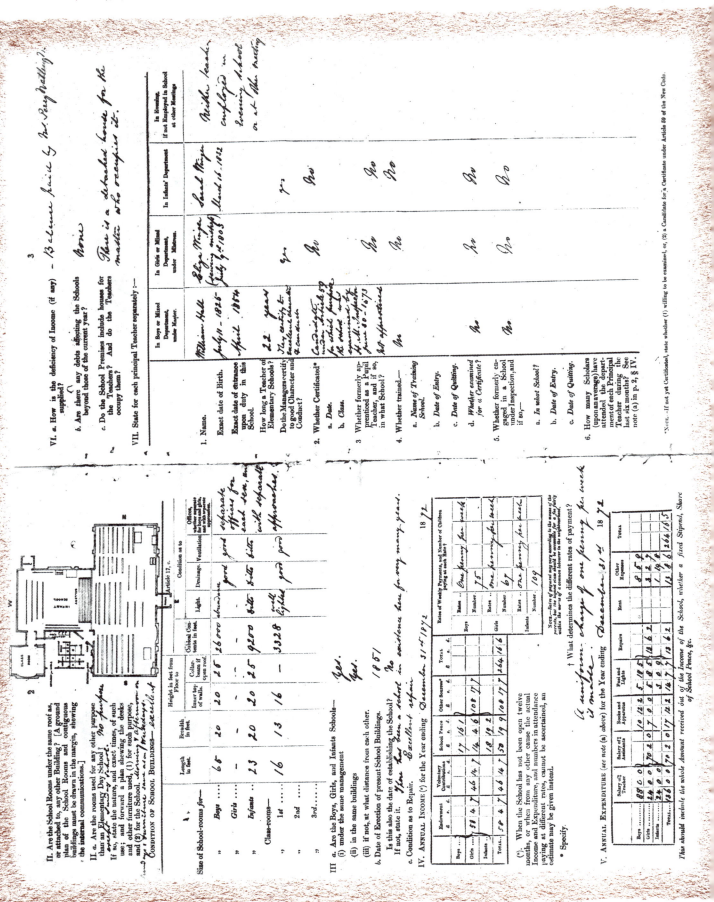

The Deluge : British Society and the First World War, contained examples of explicit quantification. We have drawn a sample of 156 lines and found examples of explicit quantification in thirty-eight of them. In other words just about 25 per cent of the lines in our sample contained such items. From what we have said already, it is likely that the proportion of such lines in the book as a whole is going to be 25 per cent ± so-so many per cent, depending on the confidence level we are satisfied with and the efficiency of our sample. To be able to decide what this ± figure is we may use a formula which gives us the *standard error* of the sample. This is akin to the standard deviation, in that it tells us how successful we have been in representing the population within our sample. It follows that if our sample size is small we shall have more difficulty in representing all aspects of the population than if it is large. This we saw quite plainly in our exercises in Unit 2. Our sample will also have difficulty in representing all aspects of the population if there is great variability in the population.

Let us turn now to our illustration. The formula is simple, but we will adopt the method used earlier of supplying a Guide. The various stages of the calculation are explained in the Guide. The only symbol to note is $S(\hat{p})$. This stands for the standard error of the sample. Its interpretation is just like that for the standard deviation. In other words we can say, to use our illustration, that we are 95 per cent certain that the proportion of lines in the whole of Professor Marwick's book containing examples of explicit quantification is 25 per cent ± 6.96 per cent (ie *twice* the standard error of the sample). The *confidence interval* then at the 95 per cent *confidence level* is between approximately 18 per cent and 32 per cent.

A Guide to Calculation: estimating from a sample the proportion of items in a population with a given attribute

In symbols	In words	Example
$$S(\hat{p})$$ $$S(\hat{p}) = \sqrt{\dfrac{pq}{N-1}}$$	The standard error of a sample	To find the proportion of lines in a book with examples of explicit qualification on them, given the proportion in the sample is 25% (ie $\dfrac{38}{156} \times 100$)
pq	A p here stands for the proportion of sample items with the attribute and q the proportion without. The two are multiplied	$p = 25\%$ $q = 75\%$ $pq = 25 \times 75 = 1875$
$N-1$	B Subtract 1 from the number in the sample	The sample is one of 156 lines $156 - 1 = 155$
$\dfrac{pq}{N-1}$	C Divide the figure reached at the end of *Stage A* by that reached at the end of *Stage B*	$1875 \div 155$ $= 12.1$
$\sqrt{\dfrac{pq}{N-1}}$	D Take the square root of the figure reached at the end of *Stage C*	$\sqrt{12.1} = 3.48$
$S(\hat{p})$	The standard error of the sample is 3.48%	

In order to avoid intellectual indigestion we will stop this discussion of sampling at this point. At the very least it is hoped that these last few pages, and the accompanying exercises have lent support to the view strongly propounded in Unit 2 that in sampling we have a very powerful tool. Even if you yourself find the calculation uncongenial, then at least you may be prepared to admit that the ideas behind sampling – such as that of *confidence level* – are of value whenever we generalize from a limited field to a wider one. You may, on the other hand, be excited by the possibilities that sampling opens up and wish to use the technique in your project. If so, you should begin now to seek out one or more of the works listed in the annotated bibliography accompanying this block of units.

Answers to SAQs

Answer SAQ 1 fistfuls; bad; all; merely; utter; greater; dash; proclivity; main; basic; blaze; any; shortages; most of all; best; great; extend; rising; most; relatively; subheading; whole collection; not very; really; completely; more relevant; main; much; before; short; succinct; largely; ordinary; half-hearted; obvious; more; completely; in the order of importance; strong enough; correspondingly; prolongation; all sorts of; different; virtually; sort of; stress; fuller; portion; much; greatly; exaggerated; move; endless; greatest.

Answer SAQ 2 208 pages.

Answer SAQ 3 The lesson is that in an exercise like this it is impossible to assess the importance of the phenomenon into which one is researching, unless one makes some kind of frequency count. Unless one does this either one's eye lights on instances which confirm one's preconceived notions, or, if one avoids this, one's brain is unlikely to be able to assess accurately the relative importance of the various manifestations of the phenomenon. Hence, if the body of material is extensive one is almost bound to sample and in drawing this sample, one must do everything possible to avoid bias.

Answer SAQ 4

Nominal data Church membership (James Dewley was allegedly a member of the Church of England); last residence; servant; complexion; colour of hair; colour of eyes; marks etc.; observations on the state of prisoner's apparel; place of nativity; father's trade and residence; marital status of prisoner; wife or husband's residence; degree of instruction; offence; where committed; magistrate's name; 'if for trial at assizes or sessions how disposed of'; 'from whence brought'; 'Has prisoner been in the Army or Navy?' 'If so, in what Regiment or Ship?'; conduct in gaol; 'Has prisoner been in custody before?' 'If so, when, and for what offence?'

Ordinal data None as such, though quite a lot of the nominal data could be transformed into ordinal data. For example, we could use the 'trade or occupation' as a surrogate for social class and so use this information to stratify the prison population. The 'apparent state of health' data might be classified as 'good; fairly good; fair; poor; fairly poor; very poor.' A similar ordering could be made of information on 'prisoner's apparel' or degree of instruction.

Interval data Age; height; number of various items of apparel; number of children and age of youngest and oldest; date of warrant; length of sentence (though if it had been, say, 'hanging', it would have been nominal); when discharged.

Answer SAQ 5

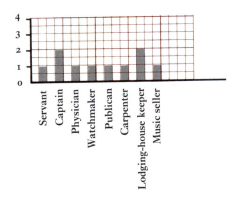

Answer SAQ 6   Class III. As the distribution is markedly bimodal, with almost all the voters in two classes (I and III) of almost equal size, the mode would be a misleading measure.

Answer SAQ 7   The distribution is bimodal, there being three values of £50 and three of £60. Since we haven't explained the calculation of the median using interval data you may not have got precisely this answer, though you should have been near it. If you take all the values in order, from the smallest to the largest, your list would appear like this: 11, 16, 18, 18, 20, 22, 28, 28, 30, 40, 43, 45, 45, 47, 50, 50, 50, 55, 55, 60, 60, 60, 65, 70, 75, 75, 90, 100, 110, 140. Since there are thirty observations, the half way point lies midway between the 15th and 16th observations. Had there been thirty-one observations, the midpoint would have been the sixteenth observation, since there would have been fifteen above and fifteen below it. In our case we must add together the fifteenth and sixteenth observation (50 + 50) and divide by 2, ie $\left(\frac{50+50}{2}=50\right)$. See Floud 1973 pp 78–9.

Answer SAQ 8

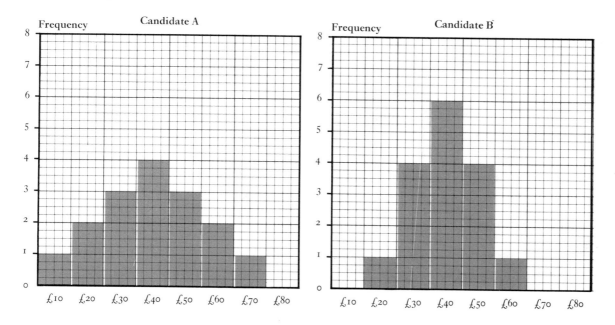

The modal, median and mean rateable value of the voters for both candidates was £40.

Answer SAQ 9   So far as the median is concerned extreme values have no more effect than those that are *just* either side of the mid-point of the distribution. As for the mode, since this is the most *frequent* observation, the outlier again has virtually no impact.

Answer SAQ 10

The standard deviation formula is:

$$\sqrt{\frac{\Sigma(X-\bar{X})^2}{N}} = \sqrt{\frac{N\Sigma X^2 - (\Sigma X)^2}{N}}$$

(a)

Stage	Symbol	Calculation
A	X^2	$50 \times 50 = 2500$ $30 \times 30 = 900$ $60 \times 60 = 3600$ $60 \times 60 = 3600$ $30 \times 30 = 900$ $80 \times 80 = 6400$ $20 \times 20 = 400$ $110 \times 110 = 12100$
B	ΣX^2	$2500 + 900 + 3600 + 3600 + 900 + 6400 +$ $400 + 12100 = 30400$
C	$N\Sigma X^2$	$8 \times 30400 = 243200$
D	ΣX	$50 + 30 + 60 + 60 + 30 + 80 + 20 + 110$ $= 440$
E	$(\Sigma X)^2$	$(440)^2 = 193600$
F	$N\Sigma X^2 - (\Sigma X)^2$	$243200 - 193600 = 49600$
G	$\sqrt{N\Sigma X^2 - (\Sigma X)^2}$	$\sqrt{49600} = 222.7$
H	$\sqrt{\dfrac{N\Sigma X^2 - (\Sigma X)^2}{N}}$	$\dfrac{222.7}{8} = 27.8$

$$S = 27.8$$

(b)

Stage	Symbol	Calculation	
A	X^2	$40 \times 40 = 1600$ $60 \times 60 = 3600$ $10 \times 10 = 100$ $50 \times 50 = 2500$ $30 \times 30 = 900$ $30 \times 30 = 900$ $20 \times 20 = 400$ $70 \times 70 = 4900$	$50 \times 50 = 2500$ $20 \times 20 = 400$ $30 \times 30 = 900$ $40 \times 40 = 1600$ $60 \times 60 = 3600$ $40 \times 40 = 1600$ $40 \times 40 = 1600$ $50 \times 50 = 2500$
B	ΣX^2	$1600 + 3600 + 100 + 2500 + 900 + 900 + 400$ $+ 4900 + 2500 + 400 + 900 + 1600 + 3600$ $+ 1600 + 1600 + 2500 = 29600$	
C	$N\Sigma X^2$	$16 \times 29600 = 473600$	
D	ΣX	$40 + 60 + 10 + 50 + 30 + 30 + 20 + 70 + 50$ $+ 20 + 30 + 40 + 60 + 40 + 40 + 50 + = 640$	
E	$(\Sigma X)^2$	$(640)^2 = 409600$	
F	$N\Sigma X^2 - (\Sigma X)^2$	$473600 - 409600 = 64000$	
G	$\sqrt{N\Sigma X^2 - (\Sigma \bar{X})^2}$	$\sqrt{64000} = 253$	
H	$\sqrt{\dfrac{N\Sigma X^2 - (\Sigma X)^2}{N}}$	$\dfrac{253}{16} = 15.8$	

$$S = 15.8$$

(c)

Stage	Symbol	Calculation
A	X^2	

$$20 \times 20 = 400 \qquad 30 \times 30 = 900$$
$$40 \times 40 = 1600 \qquad 40 \times 40 = 1600$$
$$30 \times 30 = 900 \qquad 40 \times 40 = 1600$$
$$50 \times 50 = 2500 \qquad 30 \times 30 = 900$$
$$60 \times 60 = 3600 \qquad 30 \times 30 = 900$$
$$50 \times 50 = 2500 \qquad 50 \times 50 = 2500$$
$$50 \times 50 = 2500 \qquad 40 \times 40 = 1600$$
$$40 \times 40 = 1600 \qquad 40 \times 40 = 1600$$

B ΣX^2

$$400 + 1600 + 900 + 2500 + 3600 + 2500 + 2500 + 1600 + 900 + 1600 + 1600 + 900 + 900 + 2500 + 1600 + 1600 + = 27200$$

C $N\Sigma X^2$ $16 \times 27200 = 435,200$

D ΣX

$$20 + 40 + 30 + 50 + 60 + 50 + 50 + 40 + 30 + 40 + 40 + 30 + 30 + 50 + 40 + 40 + = 640$$

E $(\Sigma X)^2$ $(640)^2 = 409,600$

F $\sqrt{N\Sigma X^2 - (\Sigma X)^2}$ $435,200 - 409600 = 25600$

G $\sqrt{N\Sigma X^2 - (\Sigma X)^2}$ $25600 = 160$

H $\dfrac{\sqrt{N\Sigma X^2 - (\Sigma X)^2}}{N}$ $\dfrac{160}{16} = 10$

$$S = 10$$

Answer SAQ 11

$$\mu = \overline{X} \pm 2\sqrt{\dfrac{S}{N-1}}$$

Stage	Symbol	Calculation
A	$\overline{X}$	From Answer to SAQ10 of Unit 2: $\overline{X} = 36$
B	S	35.4 (See separate calculation below)
C	$N-1$	$236 - 1 = 235$
D	$\sqrt{N-1}$	$\sqrt{235} = 15.3$
E	$\dfrac{S}{\sqrt{N-1}}$	$\dfrac{35.4}{15.3} = 2.3$
F	$\dfrac{S}{2\sqrt{N-1}}$	$2 \times 2.3 = 4.6$

$$\mu = 36 \pm 4.6$$

Systematic sample of Tite voters

		X^2			X^2
			Christopher Ballinger £40		1600
			George Barnes	£16	256
William Abraham	£36	1296	James Henry Barnett	£32	1024
James Aldous	£38	1444	Thomas Barter	£59	3481
Richard Allen	£70	4900	George Basson	£28	784
Henry Amor	£20	400	Charles Thomas		
Henry Archer	£25	625	Beavis	£10	100
William Ash	£25	625	William Beezley	£10	100
Abraham Aymer	£14	196	Samuel Bennett	£204	41616
George Bailey	£17	289	Thomas Biles	£60	3600
William Henry Baker	£14	196	James Bishop	£10	100
	£259	9971		£469	52661

James Blackwell	£15	225	Joseph Davis	£17	289
James Bodman	£18	324	Wm. Davis	£105	11025
Thomas Bottle	£31	961	Wm. Debank	£17	289
Edward Bowen	£16	256	Wm. Densem	£50	2500
John Bracher	£20	400	John M. Shum Dill	£20	400
John Brett	£65	4225	Wm. Dowdney	£60	3600
Thomas Brimmell	£90	8100	James Dredge	£19	361
Charles Britten	£10	100	Samuel Dudfield	£35	1225
Charles Brooke	£30	900	Robert Dunham	£16	256
Felix Brown	£55	3025	Wm. Edey	£17	289
	£350	18516		£356	20234
			Richard Passmore		
			Edwards	£30	900
Eugene Browne	£40	1600	Joseph Emerson	£25	625
Richard Bryant	£10	100	Evan Evans	£36	1296
George Buckingham	£16	256	Thomas Benjamin		
William Bullen	£32	1024	Evill	£13	169
Aaron Burton	£20	400	John Fare	£35	1225
Wm. Bush	£235	55225	Henry Fisher	£45	2025
James Buvington	£22	484	Wm. Flower	£10	100
Meshach Carey	£18	324	Solomon Francis	£50	2500
John Cartland	£24	576	Arthur Lake Fry	£50	2500
Wm. Chamberlain	£20	400	Alfred Smith		
Robert Chave	£28	784	Fulljames	£50	2500
	£465	61173		£344	13840
Henry Young					
Chiverton	£30	900	Henry Gardiner	£16	256
Samuel Churchill	£85	7225	James Gay	£30	900
Charles Clark	£28	784	Charles Gibbs	£28	784
Josias Clement	£10	100	Thomas Gill	£60	3600
John Coakley	£30	900	John Gillman	£18	324
John Cody	£27	729	Isaac Turner Glendell	£16	256
Uriah Cole	£14	196	Wm. Glover	£30	900
Edward Collins	£35	1225	Isaac Golledge	£50	2500
Nicholas Connett	£11	121	Edward Gough	£10	100
Thomas Cook	£50	2500	Joseph Govey	£13	169
	£320	14680		£271	9789
			Daniel Green	£23	529
John Cooper	£12	144	John Greenland	£12	144
Jesse Corbould	£60	3600	Wm. Gregory	£21	441
George Cottle	£28	784	John Gummer	£23	529
John Coward	£10	100	Lawrence James		
Wm. Abraham Cox	£45	2025	Hales	£45	2025
Lionel Cross	£140	19600	Thomas Hall	£50	2500
John Curry	£28	784	Edward Hancock	£120	14400
Giles Dagg	£10	100	James Harding	£18	324
Wm. Davidson	£10	100	Charles A. Harries	£40	1600
Horatio Davis	£100	10000	Thomas Harris	£18	324
	£443	37237		£370	22816

X² (cont.) X² (cont.)

Thomas Harttree	£70	4900	Henry Martin	£35	1225
Wm. Hayman	£17	289	Elias M. Matthews	£16	256
Mark Healey	£23	529	Frederick Maybury	£100	10000
James Hewett	£40	1600	Richard Melluish	£18	324
James Highfield	£31	961	Henry Paget		
Robert Hillier	£37	1369	Meredith	£67	4489
John Hodges	£36	1296	Wm. Millage jnr.	£12	144
James Holman	£14	196	Richard Mills	£16	256
Francis Hooper	£24	576	John Milsom	£27	729
Thomas Spencer			George Moger	£115	13225
Hooper	£20	400	Benjamin Moor	£45	2025
	£312	12116		£451	32673

			James Morgan	£45	2025
			Thomas Mortimer	£13	169
John Eykyn Hovenden	£80	6400	John Murley	£23	529
David Howell	£10	100	George Nation	£40	1600
Isaac Humphries	£10	100	Thomas Newman	£10	100
John L. Huntley	£15	225	Wm. Newton	£14	196
James Ingles	£25	625	Isaac Nokes	£63	3969
James Jeffery	£50	2500	George Northmore	£65	4225
Samuel Jennings	£13	169	Joseph James		
Abraham Jones	£12	144	Oldland	£65	4225
Wm. Jones	£10	100	Henry Alexander		
Alfred Keene	£25	625	Ormsby	£60	3600
	£250	10988		£398	20638

Wm. Kelly	£10	100			
James Kethro	£14	196	George Packer	£10	100
Charles King	£19	361	Thomas Palmer	£75	5625
John Kingham	£12	144	John Walker Parker	£25	625
James Knight	£10	100	Thomas Parsons	£27	729
Edward Lacey	£35	1225	James B. Pearce	£40	1600
George Wm.			George Penny	£35	1225
Langridge	£122	14884	John Perryman	£16	256
George Lansdown	£45	2025	Wm. Phillips	£19	361
Abraham Lawrence	£56	3136	Francis Pile	£80	6400
Arthur Lee	£16	256	George Pitman	£20	400
	£339	22427		£347	17321

George Lewis	£10	100	Isaac Pointing	£10	100
Wm. Lewis	£39	1521	George Popejoy	£40	1600
Charles Little	£10	100	Edward Pratt	£15	225
Ezekiel Lock	£16	256	Rice Price	£35	1225
Joseph Longman	£45	2025	Richard Punter	£16	256
John Lucas	£26	676	Wm. Ramsay	£15	225
Thomas Lye	£20	400	Sydney Alfred		
Charles Stanmore			Read	£20	400
Mager	£90	8100	Benjamin Richardson	£40	1600
Frederick Manning	£19	361	Robert Ridout	£30	900
John Mardon	£10	100	Henry Robjohn	£15	225
	£285	13639		£236	6756

Thomas Whittaker		
Rose	£140	19600
Wm. Ruddock	£10	100
James Russell	£17	289
George Salisbury	£30	900
John Sandall	£20	400
Thomas Sartain	£17	289
Richard Scain	£11	121
John Scovell	£70	4900
Charles Sendall	£11	121
Joseph Shenstone	£27	729
	£353	27449

John Sherwood	£135	18225
Henry Simester	£17	289
Joseph Simpkins	£25	625
Robert Skeates	£20	400
Thomas Slade	£10	100
George Smallcombe	£17	289
James Smith	£28	784
Wm. Smith	£60	3600
Robert Smy	£16	256
James Southey	£14	196
	£342	24764

John Stafford	£31	961
Mechiah Steer	£17	289
Matthew Stephens	£18	324
Edwin Stockman	£22	484
Henry Stothert	£100	10000
Henry Street	£175	30625
Thomas Sydenham	£12	144
Thomas Tanner	£12	144
George Taylor	£80	6400
Robert Taylor	£18	324
	£485	49695

Wm. Thomas	£20	400
Wm. Titley	£134	17956
Joseph Triggs	£18	324
Wm. Mills Trude	£30	900
John Tucker	£18	324
Charles Tutton	£200	40000
Frederick Vaughan	£25	625
George Vicker	£23	529
Thomas Vivian	£12	144
Thomas Wakefield	£12	144
	£492	61346

Robert Christie		
Ward	£120	14400
John Warren	£12	144
Stephens Watkins	£14	196
George Weaver	£45	2025
James Weeks	£16	256
John West	£10	100
Thomas Whitaker	£19	361
John White	£40	1600
Wm. Whittick	£12	144
George Williams	£12	144
	£300	19370

Joseph Williams	£45	2025
Daniel Wilton	£20	400
Godfrey Windmill	£10	100
Solomon Wolfe	£16	256
George Wood	£130	16900
Joseph Young	£26	676
	£247	20357

Grand totals $\Sigma X =$ £8484 $\Sigma X^2 = 600456$

ΣX (Total) $=$ £8484

Mean $= \dfrac{£8484}{236} = £36$

To find the Standard Deviation of the sample:—

$$S = \sqrt{\frac{\Sigma(X - \bar{X})^2}{N}} = \sqrt{\frac{N\Sigma X^2 - (\Sigma X)^2}{N}}$$

$$= \sqrt{\frac{236(600456) - (8484)^2}{236}}$$

$$= \sqrt{\frac{141707616 - 71978256}{236}}$$

$$= \sqrt{\frac{69729360}{236}} = \frac{8350}{236}$$

$$S = 35.4$$

EXAMINATION SCHEDULE. (R.)

St. Clement Danes Charity (Girls) School.

Middlesex — County.

N.B.—In order to save time, and trouble, on the day of Examination, it is requested that this Schedule may be filled up according to the directions below, before the date appointed for the Inspector's visit. It should be ready for him on his arrival at the School.

	Standard I. 1870.	Standard I. 1871.	Standard II. 1871.	Standard III. 1871.	Standard IV. 1871.	Standard V. 1871.	Standard VI. 1871.
Reading ...	Narrative in monosyllables.	One of the Narratives next in order after monosyllables in an elementary reading book used in the school.	A short paragraph from an elementary reading book.	A short paragraph from a more advanced reading book.	A few lines of poetry or prose.	A short ordinary paragraph in a newspaper, or other modern narrative.	To read with fluency and expression.
Writing ...	Form on blackboard or slate, from dictation, letters, capital and small, manuscript.	Copy in manuscript character a line of print, and write from dictation a few common words.	A sentence from the same book, slowly read once, and then dictated in single words.	A sentence slowly dictated once by a few words at a time, from the same book.	A sentence slowly dictated once, by a few words at a time, from a reading book used in the first class of the school.	Another short ordinary paragraph in a newspaper, or other modern narrative, slowly dictated once by a few words at a time.	A short theme or letter, or an essay paraphrase.
Arithmetic ...	Form on blackboard or slate, from dictation, figures up to 20; name at sight figures up to 20; add and subtract figures up to 10; orally, from examples on blackboard.	Simple addition and subtraction of numbers of not more than four figures, and the multiplication table, to multiplication by six.	The multiplication table, and any simple rule as far as division.	Compound rules (money).	Compound rules (common weights and measures).	Practice or bills of parcels.	Proportion, and vulgar or decimal fractions.

DIRECTIONS FOR FILLING IN THE SCHEDULE.

1. Children from 6 to 8 years of age are to be presented in Standard I. of the Code of 1870. Those from 8 to 10 in Standard of the Code of 1871, and those above 10 in Standard II. (or a higher Standard) of the same Code (1871).
2. The names should be entered, beginning with the lowest Standard.
3. There should be no intermixture of Standards.
4. Infants below 6 must be entered together after *all the rest in the same School* under a line.

Number	NAME	Age (on last birthday)	Under what standard (I., II., III., &c.,) to be examined	Examined and passed in ‡ Reading	Writing	Arithmetic	Special Subjects No. 1	No. 2	Number
1	Eliza Laurence	7 8	I RC	0	0	0			1
2	Mary Davert	6	"	0	0	0			2
3	Ellen Woods	7	"	x	x	x	1	1	3
4	Caroline Irwin	6	"	0	0	0			4
5	Alice Silks Button	7	"	0	0	x			5
6	Rebecca Winch	6	"	x	0	0			6
7	Cicillia Smith	7	"	0	0	0			7
8	Emily Otterman	6	"	x	x	x	1	1	8
9	Kate Spooner	7	"	0	0	x			9
10	Henrietta Irwin	8	"	0	0	x			10
11	Alice Taylor	8	I. NC	0	0	0			11
12	Lydia Kate	9	"	0	0	0			12

Number of passes carried forward ..

Part cover: Page from 1871 school inspector's report. It gives examination results for each pupil in various subjects. Source: Public Record Office, E3/27/21

Contents Unit 4

Objectives

After studying this unit you should be able to:

1 Explain in your own words what 'correlation' means.

2 Given a set of data, draw a scatter diagram.

3 Distinguish examples of correlation in which φ, r_s r_{tet} would be appropriate.

4 Using the Guides provided, calculate:
  a a mean square contingency coefficient φ;
  b a Spearman's rank order correlation coefficient, r_s;
  c a tetrachoric correlation coefficient, r_{tet};
  and give an interpretation of the coefficients calculated.

5 Describe briefly five possible sources of distortion of the calculated from the true relationship between two variables, and from the course reader (Drake 1973) give examples of three of them.

Correlation

1 Introduction

If I've been at all successful with these first few units then, by now, you should feel that quantitative techniques could well play a role in your project work. How important that role will be depends partly on your own inclinations and partly on the objectives of your enquiry and the material you draw upon. At the very least I hope that if you choose *not* to use quantitative techniques you will do so consciously, making explicit your reasons for not doing so and, where appropriate, indicating the effect, beneficial or otherwise, this decision has had upon your findings. At the other extreme you may choose to go well beyond what we have been discussing in these introductory units, or what emerges from the rest of the course. Further techniques can be got from Floud (1973) and from other works in the annotated bibliography at the end of this block of units. Most people I imagine will probably choose to operate between these two extremes. It will be interesting to see whether the distribution turns out to be positively or negatively skewed or symmetrical!

In this unit I shall be dealing with yet another way of summarizing information but whereas up to now we have been dealing with only one *variable*, here I shall be dealing with 'the discovery, measurement and interpretation of the statistical relationships between two variables' (Dollar and Jensen 1970 p 56). Partly for purposes of variety and partly because of its proved success elsewhere, some of this unit is in the form of a self-instructional text.[1] You will see that the text consists of short passages of new information, which are followed by self-test questions, and then by the answers to those questions. You may find it useful to use a postcard, or something similar, to cover up the answers to the questions, until you are ready to check the answers that you yourself have arrived at.

> A variable is a characteristic which is common to several events or phenomena, the *value* of which may vary between each *observation*. For example, during this course we hope to make eight assessments (*observations*) of your ability to do written work (*the variable*) and so obtain eight grades (*values*) for each conscientious (*sic!*) student.

2 What we mean by a correlation

When we look at the world around us we see events which often seem to happen in association with other events. Sometimes the connection seems quite clear to us, eg

A	B
Length of journey	Time taken
Size of house	Rateable value
Age	Expectation of life
Rainfall	Level of water in rivers

Questions

> 1 Are the items in A *often* directly connected with the corresponding items in B?
> 2 Are the items in B *always* directly connected with the corresponding items in A?

Answers

> 1 Yes, very often.
> 2 No, not always *directly* connected. A short journey can take a long time; the size of a house is only one factor in its rateable value; sex and occupation can be shown to affect the expectation of life; melting snow, and not rainfall, causes great changes in the level of some rivers.

---

[1] Those of you who attended the Summer School for the Foundation Course in Social Sciences in 1972 will recognize certain of the passages. These were written by Brendan Connors of the Open University Institute of Educational Technology. I am grateful to him for allowing me to use them here.

Sometimes things may seem to happen together quite regularly although there is no direct connection between them whatsoever, eg

A	B
Odd-numbered years	Above-average French wines
The beginning of the OU year	A national strike
Wimbledon	Dry, warm weather

Questions

My alarm clock rings each weekday as the announcer says 'Farming Today'.
3 Is this cause and effect?
4 Is there any connection at all between these regular co-occurrences?

Answers

3 No!
4 Yes – a convenient time to broadcast to farmers happens to be about the same time as an individual's reveille.

So when things happen together it may be because there is some connection between them, or it may be sheer chance. Even when there is a connection it is quite unsafe to conclude that it is a case of cause and effect, eg The cock mounted the dunghill and crowed. The sun came up. 'Look what I've just done!' said the cock.

Question

5 What is the disease which can be shown to be associated quite closely with a certain human addiction?

Answer

5 Lung cancer and smoking. Smokers often point out, correctly if not wisely, that the powerful statistical evidence does not prove that smoking is *causing* lung cancer.

In studying human behaviour we often need to calculate the strength of the connection between two sets of happenings, but always remembering that even a clear connection does not necessarily indicate cause and effect, or indeed anything but sheer chance. When we investigate this sort of connection we sometimes say that we are looking for a correlation and the result of our calculations is called a COEFFICIENT OF CORRELATION.

Questions

6 Is there a correlation between the amount that trees in Brighton sway about and the height of the waves off the pier?
7 Does the swaying of the trees *cause* the rough seas? Or vice versa?

Answers

6 Yes, probably.
7 Clearly not.

When two sets of happenings or measurements are directly connected in a constant proportion to each other, eg the number of pence in any given number of pounds – we have what is called a PERFECT POSITIVE CORRELATION where the

CORRELATION COEFFICIENT $= +1.0$

Since this is *perfect* correlation, the correlation coefficient can never be greater than $+1.0$.

Question

8 In which one of the following cases is the coefficient of correlation likely to be nearest to $+1.0$?
  A Age of baby/size of baby
  B Total income/amount of tax paid
  C Number of cinema tickets sold/the number in the audience
  D Number of units consumed/amount of electricity bill

Answer

8 Probably C. Babies vary in size; income tax depends upon allowances as well as income; units of electricity do not all cost the same.

Such perfect correlations are very rare indeed. When we calculate a coefficient of correlation we usually expect it to be less than $+ 1.0$. Much lower figures can still tell us quite a lot, eg

  if coefficient of correlation (amount of spinach eaten: amount won on football pools) $= +0.6$

we would be seeing queues outside the greengrocers. Even a correlation of $+ 0.2$ between A and B suggests that there is a slight tendency for B to increase as A increases and vice versa.

Question

9 Which of the following values for the coefficient of correlation between miles travelled and first-class ordinary fare paid is most likely to be correct?
  A $+ 0.3$ B zero   C $- 0.1$
  D $+ 0.1$ E $+ 0.9$ F $- 0.9$
  G $- 0.4$

Answer

9 E, $+ 0.9$ is most likely, because usually (but not quite always) the first-class ordinary fare is directly related to the distance travelled.

Sometimes events or measurements are clearly associated with each other, but in a *negative* way, eg there is a calculable correlation between daily temperatures and the amount of coal sold, with the higher the temperature the lower the figure for coal sales and vice versa.

Relationships of this kind give us a negative coefficient of correlation, eg
  A $- 1.0$ (perfect negative correlation – one rises in exact proportion to the fall in the other)
  B $- 0.4$ (there is some tendency for one to rise as the other falls)
  C $- 0.1$ (the relationship is very nearly random)

10 Which of the above, A, B or C, is least likely to be met with in an Applied Historical Studies project?

Answer

10 A. Perfect correlations, whether positive or negative, would be most unlikely. This is because of the nature of investigations in this area. A correlation of $\pm$ 0.6 would be very significant indeed. In science and technology nearly perfect correlations are more common.

We can now represent the limits of the coefficient of correlation in one diagram.

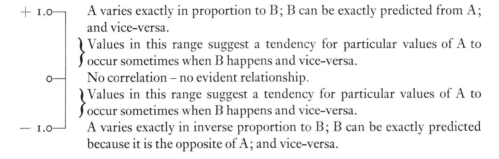

$+$ 1.0 — A varies exactly in proportion to B; B can be exactly predicted from A; and vice-versa.

Values in this range suggest a tendency for particular values of A to occur sometimes when B happens and vice-versa.

o — No correlation – no evident relationship.

Values in this range suggest a tendency for particular values of A to occur sometimes when B happens and vice-versa.

$-$ 1.0 — A varies exactly in inverse proportion to B; B can be exactly predicted because it is the opposite of A; and vice-versa.

Question

11 What would a correlation coefficient of $+$ 2.3 mean?

Answer

11 Someone has made a mistake! Coefficients of correlation must lie between $+$ 1.0 and $-$ 1.0.

Now see how much you have learnt so far.

Questions

12 If the correlation coefficient between event A and event B is 1.0, what definite conclusion can you make about a causal relationship between the two?

13 Which of these best describes a correlation coefficient of $+$ 0.5?

A A low correlation and probably of no great significance.

B A measurable and probably significant tendency for two measurements to vary in proportion to each other.

C The half-way mark between positive and negative correlation.

D A relationship only a little removed from random exists between A and B.

14 What is the coefficient of correlation between any number of years and the corresponding number of days?

Answers

> 12 No definite conclusion can be made – one could be the cause of the other, or they could be effects of the same cause, or the relationship could just be due to mere chance, however remote this probability may be.
>
> 13 B.
>
> 14 Almost + 1.0, but just a little lower, since the proportion of 1 to 365 is modified by leap years.

The coefficient of correlation is not the only way we can show the relationship between two sets of data. We can also use a kind of graph:

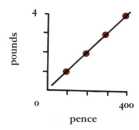

Each point on the line has a number of pounds marked up the scale to the left of it, and the corresponding number of pence on the scale below it.

Questions

> 15 How did we describe in words the kind of correlation shown by this straight line?
>
> 16 What would the coefficient of correlation be in this case?

Answers

> 15 Perfect positive correlation
>
> 16 + 1

Sometimes, though, the points do not always lie exactly on a straight line; hence the name of this kind of graph – the SCATTER DIAGRAM

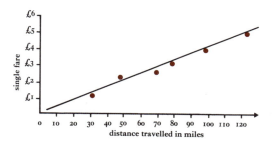

distance	fare
31	1.20
48	2.20
69	2.80
78	3.10
98	4.00
123	5.10

Question

> 17 How would you describe the correlation shown in the above diagram?
>
> A Perfect positive   D Perfect negative
>
> B High positive   E Low positive
>
> C Zero   F High negative

17 B – High positive. Because it was possible to draw a straight line which was close to all the points.

In practice we often find points scattered in these characteristic shapes.

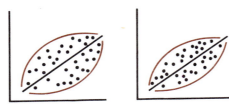

These both represent positive correlations, ie the further to the right you go the higher you get.

Question

18 Which is the higher of the two correlations, A or B?

Answer

18 B – because the scatter of points is nearer to the straight line which represents perfect correlation.

This is a fairly high positive correlation but sometimes the line slopes the other way and sometimes the points do not even roughly fall along a line.

Questions

19 Which of the following correlations is represented in Y?
   A Low positive   C High positive   E Zero correlation
   B Low negative   D High negative
20 And which of the above do you think is shown in Z?

Answers

19 D High negative
20 E Zero

If you got both these answers right you are doing very well; if you didn't, don't worry – here are the explanations.

When one thing seems to get lower as the other gets higher we have a negative correlation, and the line slopes the other way.

Number of
deckchairs
hired

X   High negative correlation

Number of inches of rain

And where there is no discernible association between the two things, the points do not even vaguely suggest a straight line.

Y   Zero correlation

Question

21 Which is the most likely coefficient of correlation for X above?
     A + 0.2   C − 0.2   E 0
     B + 0.8   D − 0.8   F − 2.7

Answer

21 D, − 0.8 because X shows a *high negative correlation.* (If you selected F, − 2.7, remember that coefficients of correlation must always lie between + 1 and − 1.)

Here are some examples as a recap of what you have been doing:

Description	Coefficient	Scatter diagram or line
Perfect positive correlation	+ 1.0	
A high positive correlation	+ 0.8 say	
A low positive correlation	+ 0.3 say	
Zero correlation	0	
A low negative correlation	− 0.3 say	
A high negative correlation	− 0.8 say	

22 What would you expect the correlation between density of traffic and number of accidents to be (in words)?

Answer

22 One might *expect* it to be high and positive, but if you really needed to know what it was for any section of road, you would have to collect some data and do some calculating, at the end of which you might, or easily might not, find your expectations confirmed.

You should now be able to describe all the following examples of correlation correctly as high or low, positive or negative, or zero, etc.; eg the answer to a correlation coefficient of + 0.2 would be *low positive*.

Questions

23 'A slight tendency for A to increase when B increases.'
24 — 0.7
25 'I can't see any association either way.'
26   27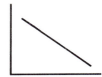

28 + 1.1.
29 Distance from Scotland/number of kilts seen.
30 Number of mice in house/number of cats kept.

Answers

23 Low positive.
24 High negative.
25 Zero.
26 High positive.
27 Perfect negative (high negative is not wrong).
28 A coefficient of correlation must lie between + 1.0 and — 1.0.
29 High negative – but your guess is as good as mine.
30 High negative – but not if the cats are senile, etc!

If you have answered all these correctly you are now in a position to begin to perform some correlation calculations, with the aid of step-by-step instructions like those in the previous unit. There are, as you might suspect, very many different ways of calculating correlation coefficients. We shall be dealing with three of these. One is used with nominal data, one with ordinal data and one with interval data. In this way they are analogous with the measures of central tendency (mode, median and mean) we discussed in Unit 3. However, unlike those measures, they all have long-winded, rather forbidding names.

3 The mean square contingency coefficient phi (φ)

Much of the data you will come across will be of the nominal type and because of this the amount of quantitative analysis you can undertake with it is comparatively slight. At one extreme you will find *dichotomous variables*, that is to say data which can be divided into two mutually exclusive categories. For example men – women; worker – non-worker; present – absent; likes – doesn't like, are all examples of dichotomous variables.

Let us suppose we want to examine the relationship between two sets of dichotomous variables. By way of illustration we've chosen to look at that between church attendance and social class. Our measure of the latter is the traditional one of manual worker – non-manual worker. It's a crude measure, (on this see Thernstrom in the course reader, Drake 1973 pp 230–1) but it will serve our purpose. We have then, let us say, 100 manual workers and 100 non-manual workers. Our exercise aims to discover whether the *differences* in the social class of our population, represented by these figures, are related to *differences* in church attendance.

We begin by setting out the data in what is called a *two-by-two table*. Look at Table 1. It is possible our data could look like this. Here none of our manual workers attended church. All our non-manual workers did so. Here is a perfect correlation, since the difference in church attendance corresponds exactly with the difference in social class.

Table 1

		X	
		Manual worker	Non-manual worker
	Church attender	0	100
Y	Church non-attender	100	0

Incidentally you will notice that in Table 1 I've introduced a little shorthand by calling one set of variables X (manual worker – non-manual worker) and the other set Y (church attender – church non-attender). Just note this for the moment. We shall come back to it later.

Table 2

		X	
		Manual worker	Non-manual worker
	Church attender	100	0
Y	Church non-attender	0	100

Now look at Table 2. Here the distribution is the *opposite* of that in Table 1. For, as you see, every manual worker attended church, but not a single non-manual worker did so. Again a perfect correlation. But is it a perfectly positive or perfectly negative one? Good question, but let's leave it for a moment. Instead turn to Table 3. Here we see 50 manual workers attending church and 50 not. We also see 50 non-manual workers attending church and 50 not. Here the proportion of church attenders (and, therefore, of non-attenders) is the same for both social groups. We have here then a zero correlation, as both groups have the same church attendance record.

Table 3

		X	
		Manual worker	Non-manual worker
	Church attender	50	50
Y	Church non-attender	50	50

Any differences there are between the groups do not, on these figures, appear to be reflected in church attendance. In the example given in Table 3 we've taken a 50:50 split; but exactly the same conclusion would be drawn, (ie zero correlation), if the

Figure 1 Examination schedule for St Clement Danes' Charity (Girls) School, 1871 (continuation of the form which appears on the cover of this unit).
Source: Public Record Office E3/27/21

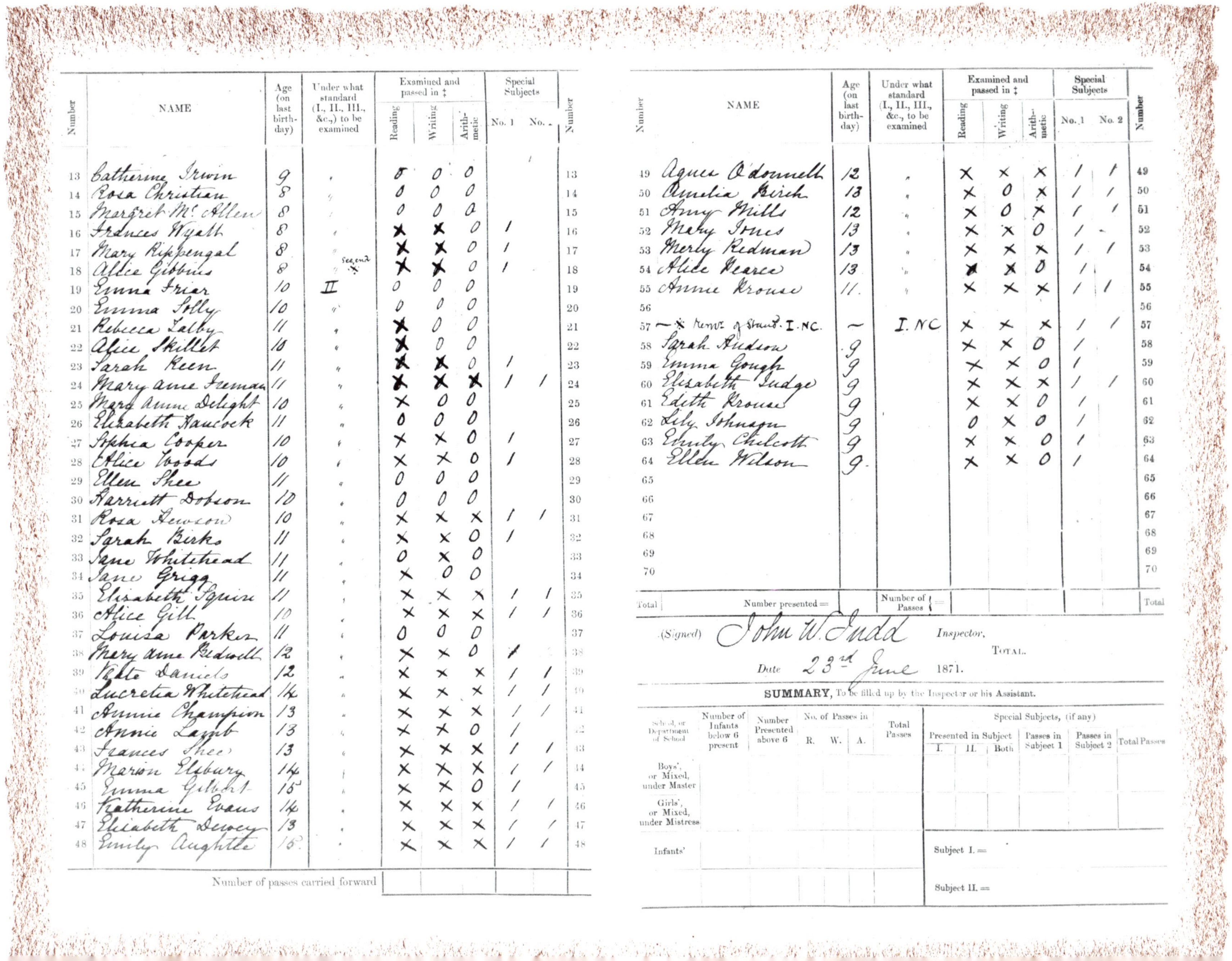

proportions had been 70:30 or 80:20 or 10:90 for both groups, or any pair of numbers you care to choose.

Let us now turn to a more realistic situation, since it's very rare to have data which falls out as neatly as that in Tables 1, 2 and 3. A more common picture is the one presented in Table 4. This shows that more non-manual workers than manual workers

Table 4

		X	
		Manual worker	Non-manual worker
	Church attender	20	70
Y	Church non-attender	80	30

attended church. On the other hand there is a minority of both manual and non-manual workers who didn't share their fellow workers' habits in this matter. So, some 20 out of 100 manual workers went to church and some 30 out of a 100 non-manual workers did not. We are somewhere, then, between a perfect correlation and a zero correlation.

Question

31 How strong do you think the correlation is, on the evidence in Table 4, between social class and church attendance?
Choose from the three ranges of correlation coefficients given below
A Between + 0.5 and + 1.0
B Between + 0.5 and − 0.5
C Between − 0.5 and − 1.0

Answer

31 A, B or C. Whichever you picked you were right. Happy thought! Technically the answer is − 0.5, but before explaining how one can square that with A, B and C being right, let us turn to the calculation of φ.

The value of − 0.5 given above was obtained by using the formula for measuring the strength of association between two dichotomous variables. This is called the *mean square contingency coefficient phi* (pronounced 'fie') and represented by the symbol φ
Here is the formula in symbols.

$$\varphi = \frac{ad - bc}{\sqrt{(a + c)(b + d)(a + b)(c + d)}}$$

To put that into words we need to go back to our two-by-two table. You may remember that, a few paragraphs back, I spoke of using a bit of shorthand by calling one set of variables *X* and the other *Y*. To simplify the explanation in the next few paragraphs

Table 5

	X		Total
	a	b	(a + b)
Y	c	d	(c + d)
Total	(a + c)	(b + d)	

I'm going to use a bit more shorthand. So I've given each cell in the two-by-two table an identifying letter as in Table 5. In words then, the correlation coefficient *phi* is:

φ = The number in cell *a* multiplied by the number in cell *d*, *minus* the number in cell *b* multiplied by the number in cell *c*

————————————————————— divided by —————————————————————

The square root of the product of the number in cell *a* added to the number in cell *c*, multiplied by the number in cell *b* added to the number in cell *d*, multiplied by the number in cell *a* added to the number in cell *b*, multiplied by the number in cell *c* added to the number in cell *d*.

I suggest you now turn to the first of three Guides to Calculation, entitled 'The mean square contingency coefficient phi', on page 111. I'll be going through this step by step. The first thing we do is to put our data into the form of a two–by–two table.

Stage A in Guide
Since of our 100 manual workers only 20 attend church, this means 80 do not. So we put 20 in cell *a* and 80 in cell *b*. Of the non-manual workers 70 attend church and 30 do not. The 70 go, therefore, in cell *b* and the 30 in cell *d*.

Question

32 Complete the two-by-two table here, given that of a 100 manual workers 40 attended church and of a 100 non-manual workers 10 did so.

| | | X Workers | |
		Manual	Non-manual
Church attendance Y	Yes		
	No		

Answer

32

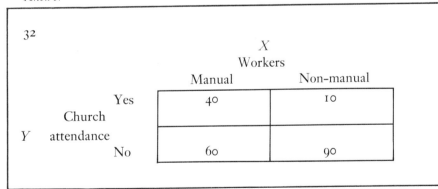

| | | X Workers | |
		Manual	Non-manual
Church attendance Y	Yes	40	10
	No	60	90

Stage B
Going back now to our example in the Guide we get 'ad' by multiplying *a* by *d*.
   $a \times d = 20 \times 30 = 600$
Stage C
To get *bc* we multiply *b* by *c*
   $b \times c = 70 \times 80 = 5600$
Stage D
To get $ad - bc$ we subtract the number calculated in Stage C from the one in Stage B
   $600 - 5600 = -5000$
You may remember from your school arithmetic that subtracting a larger number from a smaller one is done by, in effect, turning the sum round (ie subtracting the smaller from the bigger) and then putting a minus sign (—) in front of the result.

A Guide to Calculation: the mean square contingency coefficient phi

In symbols	In words	
	The mean square contingency coefficient phi.	Our population consists of 100 manual workers and 100 non-manual workers. 20 of the former and 70 of the latter go to church. How strongly are differences in social class correlated with differences in church attendance?

$$\varphi = \frac{ad - bc}{\sqrt{(a+c)(b+d)(a+b)(c+d)}}$$

In symbols		In words		
a	b	A Put the data in the form of a two-by-two table.		Manual $\times$ Non-manual workers
c	d		Y	church attenders: 20 / 70
				church non-attenders: 80 / 30
ad		B Multiply the number in cell a by the one in cell d.	$20 \times 30 = 600$	
bc		C Multiply the number in cell b by the one in cell c.	$70 \times 80 = 5600$	
$ad - bc$		D Subtract the number you obtained in C above from the number you got in B.	$600 - 5600 = -5000$	
$(a + c)$		E Add the number in cell a to the one in cell c.	$20 + 80 = 100$	
$(b + d)$		F Add the number in cell b to the one in cell d.	$70 + 30 = 100$	
$(a + b)$		G Add the number in cell a to the one in cell b.	$20 + 70 = 90$	
$(c + d)$		H Add the number in cell c to the one in cell d.	$80 + 30 = 110$	
$(a+c)(b+d)(a+b)(c+d)$		I Multiply the numbers you obtained in E, F, G and H by each other.	$100 \times 100 \times 90 \times 110 = 99\,000\,000$	
$\sqrt{(a+c)(b+d)(a+b)(c+d)}$		J Take the square root of the number you obtained in I.	$\sqrt{99\,000\,000} = 9950$	
$\dfrac{ad - bc}{\sqrt{(a+c)(b+d)(a+b)(c+d)}}$		K Divide the number you obtained in D above by that you got in J.	$\dfrac{-5000}{9950} = \approx -0.5$	
φ		The correlation coefficient phi is:	≈ -0.5	

Stage E

We now begin a series of elementary addition sums. The first one is to add the number in cell a to that in cell c.

$$a + c = 20 + 80 = 100$$

Stage F

Do the same for b and d

$$b + d = 70 + 30 = 100$$

Stage G

Repeat the operation for cells a and b

$$a + b = 20 + 70 = 90$$

Stage H

And again for cells c and d

$$c + d = 80 + 30 = 110$$

Stage I

Here we get the product of multiplying together each of the numbers calculated in Stages E, F, G and H.

That is: $100 \times 100 \times 90 \times 110 = 99,000,000$

First multiply 100 by 100, then the result of this exercise by 90, and finally the result of this by 110.

Stage J

We now need to take the square root of the number we get at the end of Stage I $\sqrt{99\,000\,000}$. There are various ways of doing this: the easiest, of course, being an electronic calculator! A slide rule is almost equally simple if one breaks the number into two parts

ie $\sqrt{99} \times \sqrt{10^6}$
$= 9.95 \times 10^3$
$= 9.95 \times 1000$
$= 9950$

Stage K
The final stage is to divide — 5000 (the figure reached in Stage D) by 9950 (the figure just calculated in Stage J)

$$- \frac{5000}{9950} = - 0.5 \text{ (or near enough: the symbol for this is } \approx \text{).}$$

Note that dividing a negative by a positive number results in a negative product.

Having got our correlation coefficient φ to be, in this case, — 0.5, you may well ask what does it mean? Well, the figure does summarize the data; it does provide us with a convenient way of encapsulating the relationship between social class (in so far as the manual – non-manual division reflects this) and church attendance. But why a *negative* correlation?

In the case of *this* correlation coefficient, the $+$ or $-$ sign is merely an artefact of the mathematics. It has no significance in terms of the relationship. That is why for Question 31, answers A, B or C were correct. For had we drawn up the table so that the data on non-manual workers had appeared in cells a and c and that for manual workers in cells b and d as in Table 6, we should have had a correlation coefficient of $+ 0.5$. The reason for this is that, whereas the data as laid out in Table 4 give a negative result ($ad - bc = (20 \times 30) - (70 \times 80) = 600 - 5600 = -5000$); as laid out in Table 6 the data give a positive one ($ad - bc = (70 \times 80) - (20 \times 30) = 5600 - 600 = + 5600$).

Our calculation has revealed a fairly strong correlation between social class and church attendance. Not *all* of church attendance can be *associated* with social class.

Table 6

	X	
	Non-manual workers	Manual workers
Church attender	70	20
Church non-attender	30	80

(Note that I use the word *associated*, not *caused*. Our correlation coefficients do not tell us what causes what, but rather what is related or associated with what. Other skills are needed for determining causation.) So we must try something else. Perhaps if we looked at some other variables, breaking down our manual – non-manual groups by say, whether male or female, whether over 50 years of age or under, we might find a stronger correlation between them and church attendance. Such is the way much of our research proceeds. Sometimes, of course, one doesn't find a final, fully satisfying answer. See for example Blumin's work in the course reader (Drake 1973 pp 233–49) with its cry from the heart on the penultimate page (p 248) – 'the Philadelphia data remain inscrutable to the last'.

SAQ 1 If you turn to Floud 1973 p 130 you will find some voting figures on the Ten Hours Bill in the House of Commons in 1844. It is possible to put these into a two–by–two table as follows:

	Party Affiliation	
Voting behaviour	Conservative	Liberal
For	100	94
Against	135	100

Use the mean square contingency coefficient phi to find out the extent to which voting behaviour can be explained in terms of party affiliation. (Note Floud uses a different method to do this which doesn't concern us at the moment.)

4 Spearman's rank order correlation (r_s)

Sometimes it is possible to rank data in a particular order even though we cannot measure precisely the intervals separating them. (You might care to refer back to Unit 3 for the discussion of nominal, ordinal and interval data.) If we wish to measure the relationship between two such rank orders we use a correlation coefficient called *Spearman's rank order correlation*; often abbreviated to *Spearman's rho* or, in symbols, r_s. To show how to calculate this we will use the method adopted for explaining the *mean square contingency coefficient phi*, and an example which you may recall from the D100 Summer School of 1972, prepared by Brendan Connors.

Let us assume we wish to find out how the accuracy of a certain group of workers correlates with the speed at which they work. We can rank them as follows:

	Rank order for speed of work	*Rank order for accuracy*
Brown	4	5
Jones	1	2
Green	5	3
Robinson	3	4
Smith	2	1

Clearly we need some way of calculating the correlation coefficient.

Question

33 Have a guess at the coefficient of correlation of the two rank orders shown above.

    A Between + 0.5 and + 1.0
    B Between + 0.5 and − 0.5
    C Between − 0.5 and − 1.0

Answer

33 A Between + 0.5 and + 1.0
    It is actually + 0.6, which means that there is a fairly high correlation between speed of work and accuracy for these individuals.

The value of + 0.6 given above was obtained by using the formula for *Spearman's rank order correlation*.

Here is the formula in symbols and underneath in words:

Symbols

$$r_s = 1 - \frac{6\Sigma d^2}{n(n^2 - 1)}$$

Words

Correlation = 1 less $\dfrac{\text{six times the sum of the rank order differences squared}}{\text{the total no of items multiplied by one less than itself squared}}$

You can see from this that the Greek letter *sigma*, Σ, is used to mean 'the sum of all the values of . . . .'

Question

34 If x has four values, 2, 3, 5 and 8, what is Σx?

School Form (No. 74 L), January, 1871.

ELEMENTARY EDUCATION ACT, 1870.

EDUCATIONAL RETURN.

DISTRICT OF THE SCHOOL BOARD OF LONDON.

Division of *Westminster*

Parish *Saint Clement Danes* Ward

Saint Clement Danes Charity School

Address (No. and Name *45 Stanhope Street*
of Street, Road, &c.)

TO THE MANAGERS, MASTER, OR MISTRESS OF THE SCHOOL.

THIS RETURN is required in pursuance of the Elementary Education Act of 1870, the object being to collect authentic information with regard to the existing provision for elementary education in the District. By the 72nd Section of that Act it is provided that, " If the managers or teacher of any school refuse or neglect to fill up the form required for the said return, or refuse to allow the inspector to inspect the schoolhouse or examine any scholar, or examine the school books and register, or make copies or extracts therefrom, such school shall not be taken into consideration among the schools giving efficient elementary education to the district

It is requested that the particulars specified may be furnished so far as the several questions are applicable to your School. This Return will be called for, and may be delivered sealed or open, with the answers written in ink in the proper columns on, or before, **the 1st March, 1871.**

If the School is a *Public* School (*see below*), the Form must be shown to the Managers, and signed by at least one of them.

If the School is an *Adventure* School (*see below*), the Master or Mistress, in case of difficulty about filling up any part of the Form, should consult the nearest Certificated Teacher.

N.B.—No Return is to be made by any School in which the ordinary Fee exceeds 9d. per Week.

I. Is the School,

i. A *Public* School; i.e., held in premises secured to be used for Education, with Managers acting under that Deed, who appoint and control the Teacher?

ii. A *Private* School; i.e., governed by Private Managers, or a Committee, not acting under any Deed?

iii. An *Adventure* School; i.e., conducted by the Teacher at his (or her) own risk, and on his (or her) own responsibility?

If the School is either (ii.) or (iii.),

To whom does the Building belong?

On what condition is it occupied?

II. With what Religious denomination (if any) is the School connected?

III. Are the School as required, or expected, to attend any special Religious Instruction, or particular place of worship?

(c) If the School has no distinctive name, it may be described by reference to the Proprietor, e.g., Mrs. Smith's School

VIII. INSTRUCTION—

How many of the children learn each of the following subjects?

	Number running	
	Day School	Night School
Reading	316	
Writing	316	
Arithmetic	316	
Dictation	203	
Religious Instruction	315	
History	63	
Grammar	103	
Geography	103	
Needlework	145	
Music—		
Vocal	70	
Instrumental	—	
Drawing	—	
Drill	—	
Other subjects, if any, specify them.		

IX. Does the School provide Instruction only? *Yes*

If not,

How many Scholars are lodged? } *30 girls*

boarded? } *30 girls*
clothed? *30 girls £10*
40 boys £10

Is the School a Ragged School, Industrial School, Reformatory, Orphanage, Asylum, or Private Boarding School? *No*

X. Has the School any Income from Endowment? *Yes*

Of what amount? *See Annexed Note*

What is the nature of the Endowment?

Is it alienable?

(1). From the School? *No See Annexed Note*

(2). From Education? *No See Annexed Note*

XI. Name and Designation (Res. or Esq. of Correspondent for School in full.)

Samuel Harvey Twining Esq.

Full postal address.

215 Strand
London
W.C.

(District Letter)

XII. I, (or we) certify the foregoing Return to be as correct as I (or we) have the means of making it.

Signed
Sam M. Twining
Thos. J. Locker } Managers, Guardians, or Trustees
W. J. Nosell
Edmund Barnes Master.
Amelia Spencer Mistress.
Infants' Mistress.

Dated this *4th* day of *February* 1871.

Form & Toy, 22, Long Acre, Printers to Her Majesty's Stationery Office.

A Guide to Calculation: Spearman's rank order correlation

In symbols	In words	Example			
r_s $$r_s = 1 - \frac{6\Sigma d^2}{n(n^2-1)}$$	The Spearman rank order correlation coefficient for		Speed	Accuracy	d	d²

In symbols	In words	Example			
		Brown	4	5	−1	1
		Jones	1	2	−1	1
		Green	5	3	+2	4
		Robinson	3	4	−1	1
		Smith	2	1	+1	1
					Σd^2	8

In symbols	In words	Example
d	A Work out the rank order difference for each item.	(see column 'd' above)
d^2	B Square each difference (ie multiply it by itself).	(see column 'd²' above)
Σd^2	C Add up all these squares, (Σ is the Greek letter *sigma*: it means 'the sum of all the . . .'.)	(see 'd²' above) 8
$6\Sigma d^2$	D and multiply by 6.	8×6 $= 48$
n	E Add up the total number of items.	5
n^2	F Square the total number of items (multiply it by itself).	5×5 $= 25$
$n^2 - 1$	G Subtract one from it.	$25 - 1$ $= 24$
$n(n^2-1)$	H Multiply the answer to G by the total number of items.	5×24 $= 120$
$\dfrac{6\Sigma d^2}{n(n^2-1)}$	I Divide the number you obtained in D above by the number you got in H (correct to one place of decimals is usually enough).	$\dfrac{48}{120} = \dfrac{2}{5}$ $= 0.4$
$1 - \dfrac{6\Sigma d^2}{n(n^2-1)}$	J Subtract the number you got in I from one. Clearly, if the value for I was more than one you have an example of a *negative* correlation.	$1 - 0.4$ $= +0.6$
r_s	The correlation coefficient	$+0.6$

Answer

> 34 $3 + 2 + 5 + 8 = 18$

As before, we will go through the calculation of this correlation coefficient step by step. If you look above you will see the Guide to Calculation: Spearman's rank order correlation.

The first thing to do is to make a table showing the two rank orders for each individual. This is done for you in the top right-hand corner of the Guide, and shows, for example, that Robinson was the third fastest and the fourth in accuracy.

Question

> 35 What is the difference between Robinson's two placings?

Answer

> 35 Robinson has gone down one place when the second column is compared with the first column, so the difference is 1. If we want to show that it is down 1 rather than up 1, we can say −1, although we don't need to do that in the present instance.

Stage A in Guide

By working out the difference in ranking for each individual we get the column marked *d* in the top right-hand corner of the Guide.

Stage B
To get the column marked d^2 you multiply each figure by itself (ie squaring it),
so we have

$d \times d$	d^2
$(-1) \times (-1)$	1
$(+2) \times (+2)$	4

Question

36 Supply the missing word in:
   We can see from the above that when we multiply two NEGATIVE numbers
   together, the answer is P — — — — — — — — — —

Answer

36 POSITIVE

Stage C in Guide
We add up all entries in the 'd^2' column in order to get Σd^2 (the sum of all the values
of d^2).

Stage D
We now need $6\Sigma d^2$, because the formula for the Spearman's rank order correlation
coefficient is

$$r_s = 1 - \frac{6\Sigma d^2}{n(n^2 - 1)}$$

To get $6\Sigma d^2$ we merely multiply Σd^2 by 6.

Question

37 If the values of d^2 were 1, 4, and 9, what would $6\Sigma d^2$ be?

Answer

37 Σd^2 is 14, so $6\Sigma d^2$ is 84.

In the example shown in the Guide, $6\Sigma d^2$ is 48.

We now set about calculating the bottom part of the fraction $\dfrac{6\Sigma d^2}{n(n^2 - 1)}$ which you

can see in the Spearman formula.

Stage E
n is the number of items in each rank order. In this example we have 5, namely
Brown, Jones, Green, Robinson, and Smith. So $n = 5$.

Stage F
We now square the number of items (multiply it by itself) $5 \times 5 = 25$. So $n^2 = 25$.

Stage G
We now need $n^2 - 1$, which is obviously 24.

Question

38 What is the significance of putting 'n' outside the bracket in $n(n^2 - 1)$?

Answer

> 38 It means 'multiply what's inside the bracket by what's outside it' – in this case multiply $n^2 - 1$ (which is 24) by n (which is 5).

Stage H

$n(n^2 - 1) = 5 \times 24 = 120$ Easy enough?

Stage I

We can now work out the fraction $\dfrac{6\Sigma d^2}{n(n^2 - 1)}$

$6\Sigma d^2$ was 48, while $n(n^2 - 1)$ was 120.

so $\dfrac{6\Sigma d^2}{n(n^2 - 1)} = \dfrac{48}{120}$

Dividing top and bottom by 24 gives us $\dfrac{2}{5}$ which, in decimals, is 0.4.

$\dfrac{6\Sigma d^2}{n(n^2 - 1)} = 0.4.$

It is usually enough to have this correct to one place of decimals.

Question

> 39 Have we finished our calculation now?

Answer

> 39 No! The whole formula is
>
> $$r_s = 1 - \frac{6\Sigma d^2}{n(n^2 - 1)}$$

Stage J

We have just seen that $\dfrac{6\Sigma d^2}{n(n^2 - 1)} = 0.4$

so $r_s = 1 - 0.4$

$= + 0.6$

We can now say that the speed of these workers correlates fairly highly with their accuracy, the correlation coefficient being $+ 0.6$.

Question

> 40 If $\dfrac{6\Sigma d^2}{n(n^2 - 1)}$ had worked out to 0.8, what would the coefficient of correlation have been?

Answer

> 40 $1 - 0.8 = + 0.2$. A low positive correlation.

Sometimes the fraction $\dfrac{6\Sigma d^2}{n(n^2 - 1)}$ works out to a value which is more than 1, in which case we have a *negative* correlation.

For example if the fraction works out to 1.3 the final stage in working out the correlation is

$$r_s = 1 - 1.3$$

Since we have to take away more than we have to start with, the answer must be *negative*; apart from that we just subtract the one number from the other, in this instance

$$r_s = -0.3$$

> 41 In your own words, what would a correlation coefficient of -0.3 between speed of work and accuracy of work mean?

Answer

> 41 (In your own words.) There is a slight tendency for speed of work to be associated with less accuracy.

If, with the aid of the Guide, you can work out the following three correlation coefficients correctly, you can feel you have mastered Spearman's rho.

Question   *Question*   *Question*

42	IQ	Maths ranking	43	Weight	Height	44	Time worked	Useful output
John	4	4	Irma	4	1	Mike	4	1
Michael	1	3	Pauline	3	4	Robert	1	4
Andrew	2	2	Gillian	2	3	Walter	2	3
Fred	3	1	Janet	1	2	John	3	2
						Peter	5	5

Answers

> 42 $r_s = +0.2$ $(\Sigma d^2 = 8)$ Low positive correlation
> 43 $r_s = -0.2$ $(\Sigma d^2 = 12)$ Low negative correlation
> 44 $r_s = 0$ $(\Sigma d^2 = 20)$ Zero correlation

As with the mean square contingency coefficient φ, finding a correlation is often only a beginning of a process, or a part of a continuing process of enquiry. In the example we worked out (correlating speed of work with accuracy of work), though the numbers were fictitious, a correlation coefficient of $+0.6$ might well have been a real one. We might then try to discover if there was any clear causal relationship here. To do that we would need to seek out further data enabling us to relate accuracy of work to such factors as say payment, age of workers, conditions at the work place and so on. In the final analysis, however, we must use our judgement. However high or low the correlation coefficient we can never say, *on the basis of that alone*, that A causes B or B causes

A. The correlation coefficient needs to be interpreted within the framework of all the relevant evidence concerning a given situation.

SAQ 2   The following example is taken from Schiller and Odén 1970 pp 143–4. Below you will see a table showing the rank order in which the names of Stalin's possible successor(s) appeared in the Russian Communist Party newspaper *Pravda* from March to June 1953. The table also gives a frequency distribution of the number of occasions on which these Russian leaders' names were mentioned in the same paper over the same period. This frequency distribution – which you may have noted is of interval data – is also (in the table) put in a rank order. What we want to find out is whether or not there is a positive correlation between *Pravda*'s unofficial ranking of the Russian leaders and the number of times their names appear in the paper. Using the data in the table calculate a Spearman's rank order correlation.

| | Rank order | |
	Pravda's listing	Number of times mentioned in *Pravda*
Malenkov	1	1
Beria	2	4
Molotov	3	2
Voroshilov	4	3
Khrushchev	5	8
Bulganin	6	6
Kaganovich	7	9
Mikoyan	8	7
Saburov	9	11
Pervuchin	10	10
Shvernik	11	5

5 The tetrachoric correlation coefficient (r_{tet})

You may remember that with interval data we were able to use several measures of central tendency (Unit 2). The flexibility of interval data is one of its great strengths. Here again we have the option of using several different correlation coefficients. Since we can often convert data into a nominal or ordinal form we can use either φ or r_s. We also have another measure which we cannot use with nominal or ordinal data, namely *Pearson's product moment correlation coefficient*, represented by the symbol r. The calculation of this coefficient is given in Floud 1973 pp 133–8, so there is little point in repeating it here. Instead I will go through one method of calculating what is called a tetrachoric correlation, represented by the symbol r_{tet}. As Dollar and Jensen (1970 pp 65–7) point out, the advantage of r_{tet} is that it is usually close to r, but takes a good deal less time to calculate. At an early stage in one's research one might then calculate r_{tet}. If the result appears to be in the hypothesized direction one can then at a subsequent date calculate r to give a more reliable and more easily interpreted measure of correlation.

The material I am using to illustrate the calculation of r_{tet} is drawn from the course reader. If you turn to p 263 you will see a table depicting the percentage Conservative vote at various elections in English borough constituencies. The material is presented in eleven regions. The exercise we are about to undertake is designed to find how strong the relationship is, across the country, between the Conservative vote at the 1880 election and that in 1885. As with previous exercises I have provided a Guide to Calculation to which I suggest you now turn (p 121). We will go through it step by step.

Stage A in Guide

First rank the regions according to percentage of Conservative vote and locate the median. Then find the number of regions that had above the median vote in *both*

A Guide to Calculation: a tetrachoric correlation

In symbols	In words	Example

		Rank**	
		1880 (a)	1885 (b)
r_{tet}	The tetrachoric correlation for		
		North	1	1

(Layout note — the Example ranking table:)

	1880 (a)	1885 (b)
North	1	1
Yorks	3	6
Lancs	6	9
E Midlands	4	2
W Midlands	7	5
Central	2	4
East Anglia	10	8
Bristol	5	7
Devon & Cornwall	8	3
Wessex	9	10
South East	11	11

$$r_{tet} = \frac{AD}{BC} \text{ or } \frac{BC^*}{AD}$$

In symbols	In words	Example
A	A equals the number of observations *above* the median in data set (a) and in data set (b)	East Anglia; Wessex; South East $A = 3$
B	B equals the number of observations *above* the median in data set (a) but below the median in data set (b)	West Midlands; Devon and Cornwall $B = 2$
C	C equals the number of observations that were below the median in (a) but above in (b)	Bristol $C = 1$
D	D equals the rest of the observations	North; Yorks; Lancs; East Midlands; Central $D = 5$
AD	E Multiply the sum calculated in Stage A by that in Stage D	$AD = 3 \times 5 = 15$
BC	F Multiply the sum calculated in Stage B by that in Stage C	$BC = 2 \times 1 = 2$
$\frac{AD}{BC} \text{ or } \frac{BC^*}{AD}$	G^* If AD is bigger than BC, the correlation is positive: if BC is bigger than AD it is negative. To find r_{tet} in each case divide BC by AD (if correlation *is* positive) or AD by BC (if it *is* negative). Then look up the values of either in the Table below. If the correlation is positive add a plus sign; if negative, a minus sign.	$\frac{BC}{AD} = \frac{2}{15} = 0.133$ The figure 0.133 is somewhere between the 0.125 and the 0.150 in the Table. The value of r_{tet} in this case is, therefore, between $+0.682$ and $+0.639$. By interpolation we can estimate it at, say, $+0.668$.

Values of r_{tet} corresponding to obtained values of BC/AD or AD/BC (whichever is smaller).

The value of r_{tet} for other values of BC/AD or AD/BC may be found by simple interpolation. All values were computed on the basis of the formulas

$$r_{tet} = \sin\left[\frac{360°A}{N} - 90°\right]$$

and

$$r_{tet} = -\cos\left[180°/(1 + \sqrt{BC/AD})\right].$$

BC/AD or AD/BC	r_{tet}	BC/AD or AD/BC	r_{tet}
.000	1.000	.225	.531
.005	.979	.250	.500
.010	.959	.275	.471
.015	.942	.300	.443
.020	.925	.325	.417
.025	.909	.350	.392
.030	.894	.375	.369
.035	.880	.400	.346
.040	.866	.450	.305
.045	.853	.500	.266
.050	.840	.550	.231
.060	.815	.600	.198
.075	.780	.700	.139
.085	.759	.750	.113
.100	.728	.800	.090
.125	.682	.850	.068
.150	.639	.900	.041
.175	.601	.950	.020
.200	.565	1.000	.000

Source: Dollar and Jensen 1970 p 69

** NB Lowest % Conservative vote = 1   Highest = 11 but we could get the same result if we ranked them in reverse order, providing both sets of data are ranked in the *same* order.

1880 and 1885. (The median per cent Conservative vote was 45.46 in 1880 and 45.8 in 1885.)

A = East Anglia: Wessex: South East = 3

Stage B   Find the number of regions whose percentage vote was above the median in 1880 but below it in 1885.

B = West Midland: Devon and Cornwall = 2

Stage C   Find the number of regions whose percentage vote was below the median in 1880 but above it in 1885.

C = Bristol = 1

Stage D   Find the number of regions that fall into none of these categories, by subtracting the sum of the totals reached in Stages A, B and C (ie $3 + 2 + 1 = 6$) from the total number of regions which is 11.

   $D = 11 - 6 = 5$

Stage E   Multiply the sum calculated in Stage A by that in Stage D

   $AD = 3 \times 5 = 15$

Stage F   Multiply the sum arrived at in Stage B by that in Stage C

   $BC = 2 \times 1 = 2$

Stage G   Divide BC by AD $= \dfrac{2}{15} = + 0.133$

Then look at the table in the Guide to convert this value to that of the corresponding r_{tet}. The figure $+ 0.133$ comes somewhere between $+ 0.125$ and $+ 0.150$. In fact it comes about $\frac{1}{3}$ of the distance moving from 0.125 to 0.150 (the difference between these two is 0.025 and that between 0.133 and 0.125 is 0.008).

So $\dfrac{0.008}{0.025} = \dfrac{8}{25} =$ about $\frac{1}{3}$

If one moves about $\frac{1}{3}$ of the way between r_{tet} 0.682 and r_{tet} 0.639 (ie $\frac{1}{3}$ of 0.043) one has 0.014 which *subtracted* (note as the value of $\dfrac{BC}{AD}$ *rises* that of the r_{tet} *falls*) from 0.682 = 0.668. At last!

SAQ 3   If you turn to Floud 1973 p 138 you will see a calculation of Pearson's product moment correlation coefficient worked out on some data showing crew size and tonnage of a number of British ships of 1907.
Using the same data find the tetrachoric correlation r_{tet}.

6 The significance of a correlation

In the previous sections we have discussed the concept of correlation and, given different types of data (namely nominal, ordinal or interval), whether or not a correlation exists and if so how strong it is. We have not discussed, except in a comparatively perfunctory fashion in Section 1, the form a relationship takes; that is to say by how much does one variable (X in our shorthand) have to change, in order to produce a change, of a particular size, in the other variable (Y). This is, however, dealt with in Floud 1973 pp 140–52, to which you may refer. Here in this final section of the unit, I want to look briefly at the *significance* of relationships. In other words can we trust the correlation coefficients we get to tell us what the true relationship between the variables is? As – with a sinking feeling! – from the very question itself, you will probably have guessed, the answer is no. In fact 'the calculated strength and form [of the relationship] may differ from the true strength and form because of five sources of distortion: *data unreliability, form misidentification, sampling error, uncontrolled variables,* and *the ecological fallacy*' (Dollar and Jensen 1970 p 90).

Most of these sources of error need not detain us. It is, for instance, quite obvious that if our data are not what they purport to be because we have made errors of 'observation, measurement, or transcription' (Dollar and Jensen 1970 p 90), then

Figure 3 Extract from Wages Book, London Brighton and South Coast Railway, 1871. Source: Public Record Office (British Rail Archives)

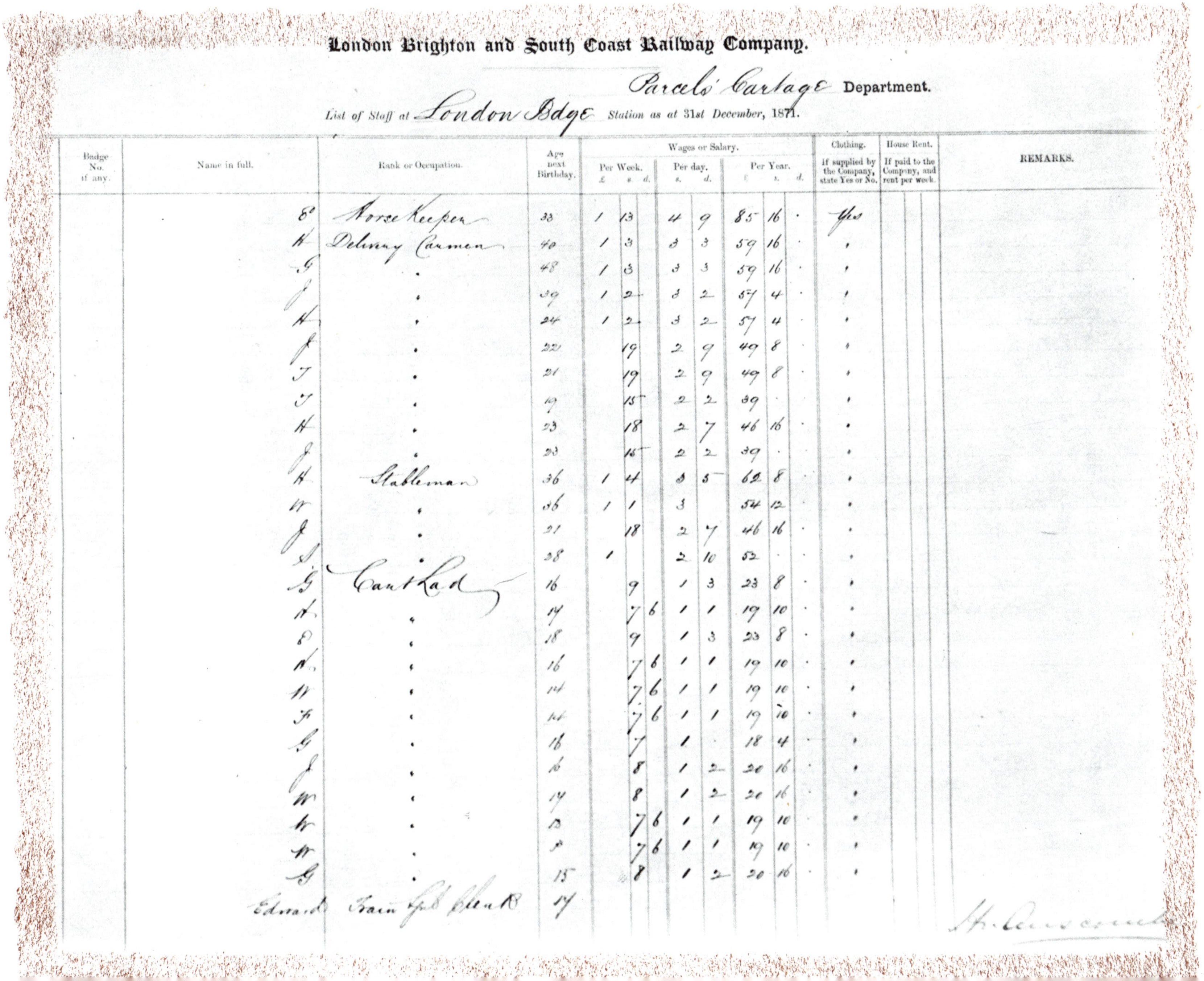

London Brighton and South Coast Railway Company.

Parcels Cartage Department.

List of Staff at London Bridge Station as at 31st December, 1871.

Badge No. if any	Name in full.	Rank or Occupation.	Age next Birthday.	Per Week £ s. d.	Per day s. d.	Per Year £ s. d.	Clothing. If supplied by the Company, state Yes or No.	House Rent. If paid to the Company, and rent per week.	REMARKS.
		Horse Keeper	33	1 13	4 9	85 16	Yes		
		Delivery Carmen	40	1 3	3 3	59 16			
			48	1 3	3 3	59 16			
			50	1 2	3 2	57 4			
			24	1 2	3 2	57 4			
			22	19	2 9	49 8			
			21	19	2 9	49 8			
			40	15	2 7	39			
			23	18	2 7	46 16			
			21	11	2 2	39 7			
		Stableman	36	1	3 5	62 8			
			45	1	3	54 12			
			21	18	2 10	46 16			
		Carman	28	1	2	52 8			
			16	9	1 3	23 8			
			17	7 6	1 1	19 10			
			18	9	1 3	23 8			
			16	7 6	1 1	19 10			
			14	7	1 1	19 10			
			18	7	1	19 10			
			10	8	1 4	18 4			
			17	8 6	1 2	20 16			
			10	7 6	1	20 16			
			8	7	1 1	19 10			
	Edward Train Girl Attend.?		15	8	1 1	19 10			
			21	9	1 2	20 16			

40872

Names in full						Date of Birth	29 June 1843
John Brown						Place of Birth	New Passage Devon

Date and Period of C. S. Engagement.	Personal Description.					Trade.	Gunnery Engagements
	Height.	Hair.	Eyes.	Complexion.	Wounds, Scars, or Marks.		
23 Apl 1863 10 years 26 & 54	5. 6	Light Brown	Grey	Dark	None	Shipwright	
23 April 1843 – 10 years		Traced					

Ships served in. Coast Guard. Seamen Riggers.	Ships' Books.		Rating, &c.	G. C. Badges worn.	Period of Service.		Time.		Character.	If Discharged. Whither and for what cause.	Remarks.
	List.	No.			From	To	Years.	Days.			
Agincourt	5	94	Shipwt	2	1 Jan. 73	28 Feb. 73					
			Caulkr Mte	„	1 Mch.	5 Augt 75			Exempy		
Indus	15ᴮ	1079	„	„	6 Augt 75				Exempt		
Impregnable	12ᵃ	27	Carp. Mte	„	1 oct.	9 oct.			Exy. 31.12.75	Exy Paid off	
	12	10	„	„	1 Apr. 76	29 Nov 76			„		
Implacable	16	196	„	Gl. 23.4.76 3	30 Nov 76	12 Dec 76			Exemp Exc 31.7.78		
Impregnable	12	10	„	„	13 Dec 76	13 Jan. 77			„		
Implacable	16	15	„	„	14 Janry 77	24 Mch 77			„		
Impregnable	12	10	„	„	25 Mch 77						
Indus	15ᴮ	703	Skilled Carp mate	„	1 May 77	5 Aug. 77			Exy Exempy		
Devastation	5	53	„	„	6 Aug. 77	19 Decy 77			Exy		
Indus	15ᴮ	1283	„	„	20 Decy 77	20 Nov 78			Vgay	C.G. £1. Lady 2r 78	
Humber	15	146	„	„	21 Nov 78	24 June 79			Exy		
Cygnet	5	12	„	„	25 June 79	7 July 79			Exy 31.12.79 V Good		
R. Adelaide	16	2635	„	„	8 July 79	31 July 83			J only	Traced P. 19 4 83	
Indus	15	1328	„	„	1 Feb 83	10 Feb 83			VGood Shore 28. 31.12.85	Pensioned D.D. 20.10.86	
Defiance	6	13	Shipwt	exempy	11 Feb 83	6 May 83					
					13 Dec 84	20 Oct 81					

whatever correlations may emerge, whether high or low, will be spurious. Again with sampling error, the same thing could occur. If we are correlating data provided by two samples it might happen that one or both of these samples may (through chance) be highly unrepresentative of the population from which it is drawn. Such an eventuality must be allowed for.

The question of what Dollar and Jensen call 'form misidentification' is another problem. It may be that the correlation coefficient one is calculating is only suitable for relationships which have a particular form or shape. For instance Spearman's *rho* is only suitable for what are called 'monotonic' relationships. A monotonic relationship is one where the values of X always increase when those of Y do so, or those of X fall when those of Y fall. If you look back at the scatter diagrams showing the relationship between the price of a single fare and the distance travelled in miles, you'll find a monotonic relationship. (You'll find this example just before Question 17). However if we were to relate the number of children per family, in this country, with the income of the parents we may get a relationship like that depicted in the figure below. This is a non-monotonic relationship in that the poorer families and the richer families have more children than the middle-income ones. For such a relationship the calculation of Spearman's *rho* (which can be used on interval data such as this, as well as on ordinal data) would give a false result.

Figure 5 Children per family according to family income: the 1960s western model.

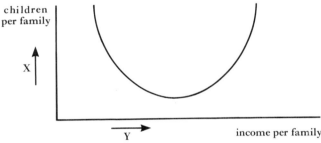

Uncontrolled variables are another cause of inaccurate correlations. For if some other factor is affecting X and Y, but in different ways, our correlation coefficient does not show what it purports to show. It is possible to allow for this, though we will not deal with it here.

The final source of distortion is the *ecological fallacy*. The source of this is that we sometimes confuse the qualities, or features of an individual with those of an area. For instance an individual is male or female, is of a certain age, votes Conservative, Labour, Liberal etc., has a particular income, a particular kind of car and so on. But areas (ie towns, parishes, counties etc) can also have attributes *as areas* – like a 20 per cent immigrant population, a median income of £2000, a mean Conservative vote of 70 per cent and so forth. The ecological fallacy arises when we make statements about individual attributes, on the basis of area (or ecological) attributes. For instance if we find the correlation between the proportion of low-income families and the proportion of large families for a number of areas is high, we might assume that poor people have large families. But this may not be so. Or again if we find that the correlation between the percentage of immigrants and the percentage of illiterates for a number of areas is high we might assume that immigrants (or a high proportion of them) cannot read or write. Again 'it ain't necessarily so!' To demonstrate this try the following exercise.

SAQ 4 Let us suppose we want to correlate the percentage voting Conservative in certain areas with the percentage of houses with a rateable value in excess of £200 in those same areas. The information on voting is readily available from Electoral returns, that on rateable values from the rating lists kept at the local government offices and open for inspection there. The results of our imaginary data collection exercise were as follows:

Town	$X = $ Percentage Conservative Vote	$Y = $ Percentage of houses with £200 + rateable values
A	20	44
B	30	46
C	40	48
D	50	50
E	60	52

To correlate the two we should use Pearson's product moment correlation, but to save time do r_{tet}, as shown above.

Having got r_{tet}, let us suppose we came, by chance, across another researcher who had been given enough money to survey *individual* householders about their voting behaviour. He too then correlated the percentage voting Conservative with percentage living in houses with a rateable value in excess of £200. His data appeared like this:

Houses of:	X Conservative voters	Non-Conservative voters	Total
Rateable value above £200 Y	1200	1200	2400
Rateable value below £200	800	1800	2600
Total	2000	3000	5000

Having set this out in a two-by-two table he then proceeded (as I now ask you) to calculate a mean square contingency coefficient phi.

Assuming you have done these calculations correctly, you will have got an r_{tet} of $+ 1.0$ and a φ of $+ 0.196$. In words this means that the ecological correlation, the one relating areas to areas, suggests that *all* Conservative voters lived in houses with a rateable value of £200 or more. The individual correlation shows that the relationship between the two was very weak indeed. The reason for the discrepancy lies in the fact that ecological data, which gives us, by definition, only area figures, may mask considerable variations in the characteristics of individuals living within them. Look, for instance, at the figures below. Here we give three widely varying figures for the *number* of Conservatives in Town 'A' with houses of a rateable value in excess of £200, but if you examine the percentage figures of the proportion of Conservative voters in the areas and the proportion of houses with a rateable value in excess of £200 you'll see they remain the same.

Hypothetical distribution of voters and household values in Town 'A'

Rateable value houses	Conservative voters	Non-Conservative voters	Total	Percentage
(i) £200 +	100	380	480	48
under £200	300	220	520	52
Total	400	600	1000	100
Percentage	40	60	100	

Rateable value houses	Conservative voters	Non-Conservative voters	Total	Percentage
(ii) £200 +	200	280	480	48
under £200	200	320	520	52
Total	400	600	1000	100
Percentage	40	60	100	

Rateable value houses	Conservative voters	Non-Conservative voters	Total	Percentage
(iii) £200 +	300	180	480	48
under £200	100	420	520	52
Total	400	600	1000	100
Percentage	40	60	100	

Answers to SAQs

Answer SAQ 1 The formula for calculating the mean square contingency coefficient is: $\varphi = \dfrac{ad - bc}{\sqrt{(a + c)(b + d)(a + b)(c + d)}}$

Party affiliations

Voting behaviour	Conservative	Liberal
For	(a) 100	(b) 94
Against	(c) 135	(d) 56

Stage	Symbol	Calculation
B	ad	$100 \times 56 = 5600$
C	bc	$94 \times 135 = 12\,690$
D	$ad - bc$	$5600 - 12\,690 = -7090$
E	$(a + c)$	$100 + 135 = 235$
F	$(b + d)$	$94 + 56 = 150$
G	$(a + b)$	$100 + 94 = 194$
H	$(c + d)$	$135 + 56 = 191$
I	$(a + c)(b + d)(a + b)(c + d)$	$235 \times 150 \times 194 \times 191 = 1\,306\,153\,500$
J	$\sqrt{(a + c)(b + d)(a + b)(c + d)}$	$\sqrt{1\,306\,153\,500} = 36\,140$
K	$\dfrac{ad - bc}{\sqrt{(a + c)(b + d)(a + b)(c + d)}}$	$\dfrac{-7090}{36\,140} = -0.2$

The correlation coefficient is − 0.2.

As explained in the text the negative sign is of no significance. What we have here then is a rather low correlation between party affiliation and voting behaviour on this particular issue.

Answer SAQ 2 The formula for calculating the Spearman's rank order correlation coefficient is: $r_s = 1 - \dfrac{6\Sigma d^2}{n(n^2 - 1)}$

Rank order

	Pravda's listing	No of times mentioned in Pravda	d	d^2
Malenkov	1	1	0	0
Beria	2	4	−2	4
Molotov	3	2	+1	1
Voroshilov	4	3	+1	1
Khrushchev	5	8	−3	9
Bulganin	6	6	0	0
Kaganovich	7	9	−2	4
Mikoyan	8	7	+1	1
Saburov	9	11	−2	4
Pervuchin	10	10	0	0
Shvernik	11	5	+6	36
			$\Sigma d^2 =$	60

Stage	Symbol	Calculation
D	$6\Sigma d^2$	$6 \times 60 = 360$
E	n	11
F	n^2	$11 \times 11 = 121$
G	$n^2 - 1$	$121 - 1 = 120$
H	$n(n^2 - 1)$	$11 \times 120 = 1320$
I	$\dfrac{6\Sigma d^2}{n(n^2 - 1)}$	$\dfrac{360}{1320} = 0.3$
J	$1 - \dfrac{6\Sigma d^2}{n(n^2 - 1)}$	$1 - 0.3 = +0.7$

The correlation coefficient is $+0.7$ which is really quite a strong one.

Answer SAQ 3 The formula for calculating the tetrachoric correlation coefficient is: $r_{tet} = \dfrac{AD}{BC}$ if the correlation is negative or $\dfrac{BC}{AD}$ if the correlation is positive

Ship No	Crew size (a)	Rank	Tonnage (b)	Rank
1697	3	21	44	24
2640	6	17	144	19
35 052	5	18	150	18
62 595	8	16	236	16
73 742	16	10	739	11
86 658	15	12	970	10
92 929	23	3	2371	4
93 086	5	18	309	15
94 546	13	13	679	12
95 757	4	20	26	25
96 414	19	7	1272	7
99 437	33	1	3246	1
99 495	19	7	1904	5
107 004	10	14	357	14
109 597	16	10	1080	8
113 406	22	4	1027	9
113 685	2	23	45	23
113 689	3	21	62	22
114 424	2	23	68	21
114 433	22	4	2507	3
115 143	2	23	138	20
115 149	18	9	502	13
115 357	21	6	1501	6
118 852	24	2	2750	2
123 375	9	15	192	17

Median crew size = 13
Median tonnage = 502

Stage	Symbol	Calculation
A	A	$A = 12$
B	B	$B = 0$
C	C	$C = 0$
D	D	$D = 13$
E	AD	$12 \times 13 = 156$
F	BC	$0 \times 0 = 0$
G	AD is bigger than BC	$0 \div 156 = \dfrac{0}{156} = 0$

Therefore the correlation is positive, and we divide BC by AD

r_{tet} from the table is therefore 1.00

Answer SAQ 4

Town	Percentage Conservative vote	Rank (a)	Percentage houses with £200 rateable values	Rank (b)
A	20	5	44	5
B	30	4	46	4
C	40	3	48	3
D	50	2	50	2
E	60	1	52	1

Stage	Symbol	Calculation
A	A	$A = 2$
B	B	$B = 0$
C	C	$C = 0$
D	D	$D = 3$
E	AD	$2 \times 3 = 6$
F	BC	$0 \times 0 = 0$
G	AD is bigger than BC, therefore the correlation is positive, and we divide BC by AD	$\dfrac{0}{6} = 0$ From the table, $r_{tet} = +1$

Rateable values	Conservative voters	Non-Conservative voters	Total
Above £200	1200 (a)	1200 (b)	2400
Below £200	800 (c)	1800 (d)	2600
Total	2000	3000	5000

The formula for calculating the mean square contingency coefficient phi is:

$$\varphi = \frac{ad - bc}{\sqrt{(a+c)(b+d)(a+b)(c+d)}}$$

Stage	Symbol	Calculation
B	ad	$1200 \times 1800 = 2\,160\,000$
C	bc	$1200 \times 800 = 960\,000$
D	$ad - bc$	$2\,160\,000 - 960\,000 = 1\,200\,000$
E	$(a + c)$	$1200 + 800 = 2000$
F	$(b + d)$	$1200 + 1800 = 3000$
G	$(a + b)$	$1200 + 1200 = 2400$
H	$(c + d)$	$800 + 1800 = 2600$
I	$(a+c)(b+d)(a+b)(c+d)$	$2000 \times 3000 \times 2400 \times 2600$ $= 37\,440\,000\,000\,000$
J	$\sqrt{(a+c)(b+d)(a+b)(c+d)}$	$\sqrt{37\,440\,000\,000\,000} = 6\,118\,823$
K	$\dfrac{ad - bc}{\sqrt{(a+c)(b+d)(a+b)(c+d)}}$	$\dfrac{1\,200\,000}{6\,118\,823} = 0.196$

$$\varphi = +\,0.196$$

Units 1-4 Annotated bibliography

The items selected for brief comment here cover the subjects discussed in Units 1-4. Those units provide, one hopes, an adequate entry behaviour for proceeding to any of the items listed, though some may prove more testing than others.

ANDERSON, M. (1971) *Family Structure in Nineteenth-Century Lancashire*, Cambridge University Press.

This is an outstanding work in the Applied Historical Studies genre. It brings together sociological theory, statistical techniques, historical data, (principally the census enumerators' books for 1841, 1851, and 1861), in order to cast light on a key problem; the 'relationship between industrialization and family structure.' Some of Dr Anderson's findings will be discussed later in the course. Parts of the book, as he admits, are 'heavy going'.

DOLLAR, C. M. and JENSEN, R. J. (1970) *Historian's Guide to Statistics: Quantitative Analysis and Historical Research*, New York, Holt, Rinehart and Winston.

This is a three-part work. The first 150 pages teach the statistical methods most appropriate for the analysis of historical data; the second 100 deal with the fundamentals of data processing and computer applications in historical research; the last 60 pages consist of a bibliographical guide to works of value in quantitative historical research. Though the authors claim to have provided 'a step-by-step introduction to all important techniques necessary for conducting serious quantitative research using historical data,' some of their 'steps' are big ones. Rather difficult.

DRAKE, M. (ed) (1973) *Applied Historical Studies: An Introductory Reader*, London, Methuen.

In this reader I have tried to show the wide variety of subject matter and technique available for exercises in applied historical studies. The topics covered range from economic growth and educational provision to voting behaviour; theory is drawn from demography, sociology, economics, psychology and genetics and statistical techniques extend from means and medians to multiple regression analysis. Because of this breadth of coverage, the reader is quite demanding in parts.

ELTON, G. R. (1967) *The Practice of History*, London, Methuen.

Professor Elton is a distinguished historian whom I would hesitate to call 'traditional', but who certainly has little love for 'new methods' or social scientists. His book is a useful counter to what I have written in Unit 1. Professor Elton's reputation is based primarily on his study of administrative changes in early Tudor government.

ELZEY, F. F. (1971) *A Programmed Introduction to Statistics*, 2nd ed. Belmont California, Brooks-Cole.

For anyone wanting a thorough and comparatively painless grounding in the statistical techniques used in this course, Elzey's programmed text can be highly recommended. It really is a step-by-step approach, with steps of an appropriate size. It is not for 'dipping into'; the whole should be taken in the order it is presented.

FLOUD, R. (1973) *An Introduction to Quantitative Methods for Historians*, London, Methuen.

Dr Floud covers somewhat less ground than Dollar and Jensen; this is especially so with his section on 'computers and data processing'. Particularly valuable are his chapters on time series and 'the problem of imperfect data', both matters of acute concern for users of historical materials. His approach is gentle; he seems to assume, probably quite rightly, that his main audience is likely to be innumerate, though it is not as gentle as the programmed texts by Elzey or McCollough and Van Atta. In terms of difficulty the book lies between what I have presented in Units 2-4 and the first half of Dollar and Jensen.

GOTTSCHALK, L. (ed) (1963) *Generalization in the Writings of History: A Report of the Committee on Historical Analysis of the Social Science Research Council*, University of Chicago Press.

Written primarily for historians, this is an important collection of articles deserving a wider currency amongst all who seek to generalize about human behaviour. It does so because, as Erikson points out in Drake 1973, social scientists are prone to ignore some of the problems of generalization; problems which the historians have faced, if only then to pass on. Particularly valuable contributions are by David M. Potter 'Explicit data and implicit assumptions in historical study'; Thomas C. Cochran 'The historian's use of social role' and William O. Aydelotte 'Notes on the problem of historical generalization'.

HARTE, N. B. (ed) (1971) *The Study of Economic History: Collected Inaugural Lectures 1893–1970*, London, Frank Cass.

As a university discipline, economic and social history has developed rapidly over the past twenty years. According to the introduction to this book there are nearly 30 professors of the subject in Britain; 200 specialist teachers in the universities alone; the Economic History Society has a membership of 3000 and its journal, the *Economic History Review* a circulation of almost 5000. Most of the lectures in the volume take up the problem of the relationship between history and the social sciences. Synthesis is not always achieved, but viewing the tension between the two, as it appears in the minds of the different authors, is an interesting experience. These lectures were prepared for non-specialist audiences and are not difficult to follow.

LANGER, W. (1973) *The Mind of Adolf Hitler*, London, Secker and Warburg.

Written by an American psychoanalyst, this work is an exercise in 'psycho-history'. In vogue in the United States, this 'new' kind of enquiry has received a cool, not to say hostile, reception amongst historians in this country. This particular example does seem highly speculative; theory (its critics say) is used to 'create' facts in a wholly unacceptable manner. Deductive rather than inductive in method, it is nevertheless a warning for students of applied historical studies.

MCCOLLOUGH and VAN ATTA (1963) *Statistical Concepts: A Programme of Self Instruction*, New York–London, McGraw-Hill.

Written originally for psychology students, and therefore using illustrations from that discipline, this programmed text is perfectly suitable for beginners of all disciplines who want an easy introduction to basic statistical techniques. In one respect it has an advantage over Elzey (1971) in that 'whole sections of the text may be studied without knowledge of other sections.' This makes access to instruction in particular techniques somewhat easier.

MEEK, R. L. (1971) *Figuring out Society*, London, Fontana.

The study of statistical methods may be a worthy pursuit; it is rarely an entertaining one. Professor Meek attempts to make it so and, remarkably, succeeds. This is not, however, a programmed text, rather an unconventional text book. The illustrations are amusing and this helps sustain the reader, but students who have great difficulty with numbers should, perhaps, use Meek in conjunction with a programmed text.

RAISON, T. (ed) *The Founding Fathers of Social Science*, Harmondsworth, Penguin.

This collection is in several ways the counterpart of Harte (1971). Like Harte it is readable; the items first appeared as articles in *New Society*. The authors are also eminent practitioners in the social sciences field, and the work as a whole does give a survey of what social scientists have been up to, mostly over the last hundred years. It is interesting to see how many of these 'founding fathers' turned to history for a part of their inspiration, eg Comte, Marx, Spencer, Weber, the Webbs, even Radcliffe-Brown, who is described as 'a-historical not anti-historical'.

SCHILLER, B. and ODÉN, BIRGITTA (1970) *Statistik för historiker*, Stockholm, Almqvist and Wiksell.

This Swedish counterpart to Floud (1973) and Dollar and Jensen (1970) ranges more widely than either and is more generously illustrated, both in the graphic sense and to a lesser degree in drawing examples from actual historical enquiries. It includes a chapter on the historical statistics available in Scandinavia, their strengths and shortcomings – despite the latter they are still the finest in the world both in terms of coverage and time-span. There is also an annotated bibliography of works on Denmark, Finland, Iceland, Norway and Sweden which use historical statistics. Though not yet translated this is a book which deserves a place in any bibliography of this kind.

SCHOFIELD, R. S. (1972) 'Sampling in historical research' in WRIGLEY, E. A.

A comprehensive account of the various sampling techniques of use on historical data. It covers the problems of drawing a sample; discusses sample size and the precision of sample estimates; how to decide the size of a sample, how to draw a pilot sample and how to estimate, from the sample, the various characteristics of the population under consideration. A bit daunting at first sight, it mellows on the second or third approach. Dr Schofield takes pains to explain each of the arithmetical operations needed to make a reality of any particular sampling exercise.

SWIERENGA, R. P. (ed) (1970) *Quantification in American History: Theory and Research*, New York, Atheneum.

This is an extremely attractive collection. As I have written elsewhere, it is 'a model of what a reader should be; judiciously edited, coherently expressed.' Although its subject matter is American history, the contributors deal with many of the problems discussed in Units 1–4; the relevance of quantification; the contributions that 'history' can make to developing general theory of social behaviour; the relationship between history and the social sciences. Contributions come from such pioneers in the field as Aydelotte, Benson, Thernstrom, Fogel and Jensen.

WISEMAN, J. P. and ARON, M. S. (1972) *Field Projects in Sociology*, London, Transworld.

This is a practical guide to the ways in which small-scale projects can be carried out by individual students or groups of students. Though it is primarily intended for sociology students, and for the study of contemporary situations, students of other disciplines and other periods will find its 'nuts and bolts' approach gratifyingly down to earth. A major concern is to show how to present qualitative and quantitative evidence and how to write up research reports. There is an extensive bibliography for each suggested project and technique.

WRIGLEY, E. A. (ed) (1972) *Nineteenth-Century Society: Essays in The Use of Quantitative Methods for the Study of Social Data*, Cambridge University Press.

This is a publication of the Cambridge Group for the History of Population and Social Structure. About three-quarters of the book is devoted to analysing the strengths and weaknesses of the population census, particularly the enumerators' returns, of 1841–91. There are also chapters on criminal statistics and education statistics, and one on sampling in historical research by R. S. Schofield (q.v.). For anyone contemplating work on the census enumerators' returns, the book is essential reading. The chapters are of varying degrees of difficulty.

Other references

This section includes full bibliographical details of works cited in the texts of Units 1–4, unless they have already been covered in the annotated bibliography above. There are also references to other works related to the subject matter of Units 1–4.

ABLER, R. et al. (1971) *Spatial Organization: The Geographer's View of the World*, Englewood Cliffs, New Jersey, Prentice-Hall.

ANDERSON, T. R. and ZELDITCH, M. (1968) *A Basic Course in Statistics With Sociological Applications*, 2nd ed. New York, Holt, Rinehart & Winston.

ARONSON, S. H. (1969) 'Obstacles to a rapprochement between history and sociology: a sociologist's view' in M. SHERIF and C. W. SHERIF (eds), (1969), pp. 292–304.

AYDELOTTE, W. O. (1971) *Quantification in History*, Reading, Mass., Addison-Wesley.

BAKER, A., HAMSHERE, R. H., JOHN, D. and LANGTON, J. (eds) (1970) *Geographical Interpretations of Historical Sources*, Newton Abbot, David & Charles.

BARTHOLOMEW, D. J. and BASSETT, E. E. (1971) *Let's Look at Figures: The Quantitative Approach to Human Affairs*, Harmondsworth, Penguin Books.

BELL, C. and NEWBY, H. (1972) *Community Studies: An Introduction to the Sociology of the Local Community*, London, George Allen and Unwin.

BIERSTEDT, R. (1957) *The Social Order*, New York, McGraw-Hill.

BRADBURN, N. M. and BERLEW, D. E. (1961) 'Need for achievement and English industrial growth' in *Economic Development and Cultural Change*, 10, 1, pp. 8–20.

CARR, E. H. (1964) *What is History?*, Harmondsworth, Penguin Books.

CONNELL, K. H. (1951) 'Some unsettled problems in English and Irish population history, 1750–1845' in *Irish Historical Studies*, 7, No 28. Reprinted in DRAKE, M. (1969).

CRAWLEY and CORCORAN (1971) 'Personality development' in BROWN, HEDY; CORCORAN, D. W. J.; CRAWLEY, ROBERTA and FINNEGAN, RUTH, *Socialization* (1971), Milton Keynes, The Open University Press.

DEPARTMENT OF EDUCATION AND SCIENCE (1973) *Statistics of Education Vol. II School Leavers CSE and GCE*, London, HMSO.

DRAKE, M. (ed) (1969) *Population in Industrialization*, London, Methuen.

FLOUD, R. (1973) *Essays in Quantitative Economic History*, Clarendon Press.

FOGEL, R. W. (1964) *Railroads and American Economic Growth: Essays in Econometric History*, Baltimore, The Johns Hopkins Press.

GALTUNG, J. (1967) *Theory and Methods of Social Research*, London, Allen and Unwin.

GOWER, N. (1973) 'Learning from figures of fun' in the *Guardian*, 12 June 1973.

GREGORY, S. (1968) *Statistical Methods and the Geographer*, London, Longman, 2nd ed.

HALPERN, B. (1957) 'History, sociology and contemporary area studies' in *American Journal of Sociology*, 63, pp. 1–10.

HUFF, D. (1967) *How to Lie with Stastistics*, London, Gollancz.

HUGHES, H. S. (1960) 'The historian and the social scientist' in *American Historical Review*, 66, pp. 20–46.

KENNISTON, K. (1968) *Young Radicals*, New York, Harcourt, Brace and World.

LAING, MARGARET (1972) *Edward Heath Prime Minister*, London, Sidgwick and Jackson.

LASLETT, P. (1968) 'History and the social sciences' in *International Encyclopedia of the Social Sciences*, 6, New York, Macmillan and Free Press, pp. 434–40.

LINDLEY, D. V. and MILLER, J. C. P. (1968) *Cambridge Elementary Statistical Tables*, Cambridge University Press.

LIPSET, S. M. and HOFSTADTER, R. (eds) (1968) *Sociology and History: Methods*, New York, Basic Books.

MADGE, J. (1953) *The Tools of Social Science*, London, Longmans.

MARWICK, A. (1963) *The Explosion of British Society 1914–62*, London, Pan Books.

MARWICK, A. (1967) *The Deluge: British Society and the First World War*, Harmondsworth, Penguin.

OHLIN, G. (1966) 'No safety in numbers', in Harry Rosovsky (ed) *Industrialization in Two Systems: Essays in Honor of Alexander Gerschenkron*, New York, Wiley.

PITT, D. C. (1972) *Using Historical Sources in Anthropology and Sociology*, New York, Holt, Rinehart and Winston.

SCHOFIELD, R. S. (1972) 'Computing, statistics and history' in *The Historical Journal*, 15, 2, pp. 325–30.

SHERIF, M. and SHERIF, CAROLYN W. (eds) (1969) *Interdisciplinary Relationships in the Social Sciences*, Chicago, Aldine Publishing Company.

SHORTER, E. (1971) *The Historian and the Computer*, Englewood Cliffs, N. J., Prentice-Hall.

SOCIAL SCIENCES FOUNDATION COURSE TEAM (eds) (1970) *Understanding Society: Readings in the Social Sciences*, London, Macmillan–Open University Press.

SOCIAL SCIENCES RESEARCH COUNCIL (1971) *Research in Economic and Social History*, London, Heinemann.

SPENCER, H. (1904) *An Autobiography*, London, Williams and Norgate.

STEPHAN, F. F. and MCCARTHY, P. J. (1958) *Sampling Opinions: An Analysis of Survey Procedure*, New York, John Wiley.

TREVOR-ROPER, H. R. (1969) 'The past and the present: history and sociology' in *Past and Present*, 42, pp. 3–17.

TUMA, E. H. (1971) *Economic History and the Social Sciences: Problems of Methodology*, Berkeley, University of California Press.

VINCENT, J. R. (1967) *Pollbooks. How Victorians Voted*, Cambridge University Press.

WEEKS, D. R. (1972) *A Glossary of Sociological Concepts*, Milton Keynes, the Open University Press.

WILSON, B. R. (1971) 'Sociological methods in the study of history' in *Transactions of the Royal Historical Society*, 5th Series, 21, pp. 101–18.

WILSON, E. K. (1966) *Sociology: Rules, Roles and Relationships*, Howard, Illinois, Dorsey Press.

Acknowledgements

Grateful acknowledgement is made to the following sources for material used in this block:

Unit 1

Figure 2a: Bucks County Records Office; *Figure 2b*: Banbury Public Library; *Figures 3 and 4*: copies of Crown-copyright records in the Public Record Office used by permission of the Controller, HMSO; *Figure 5*: from R. W. Fogel, *Railroads and American Economic Growth*, copyright © 1964 The Johns Hopkins University Press; *Figure 6*: Martin Secker & Warburg Ltd for G. Rudé, *Hanoverian London, 1714–1808*.

Unit 2

Appendix 1: Department of Statistics & Computer Science, University College London for the random numbers from D. V. Lindley and J. C. P. Miller, *Cambridge Elementary Statistical Tables* (Cambridge University Press) which were originally published in *Tracts for Computers No. 24*. *Figure 1*: Aylesbury County Record Office; *Figures 2 to 6 and part cover*: Reproductions of Crown-copyright material in the Public Record Office used by permission of the Controller of H.M. Stationery Office.

Unit 3

A. D. Peters and Company for A. Marwick, *The Deluge*, reprinted by permission. *Figures 1, 3, 10, 11 and part cover*: Reproductions of Crown-copyright records in the Public Record Office used by permission of the Controller of H.M. Stationery Office; *Figure 2*: City and County Borough of Bath.

Unit 4

Tables in SAQ 2: Almqvist & Wiksell for Schiller and Odén, *Statistik för Historiker*. *Figures 1, 2, 3, 4 and part cover*: Reproductions of Crown–copyright records in the Public Record Office used by permission of the Controller of H.M. Stationery Office.

Historical data and the social sciences

Block one   The quantitative analysis of historical data
Unit 1   Words and numbers, sources and theory
Unit 2   Sampling
Unit 3   Describing data
Unit 4   Correlation

Block two   Historical demography: problems and projects
Unit 5   Population and economy
Unit 6   Population and society
Unit 7   *La crise démographique*
Unit 8   Migration

Block three   Introduction to historical psephology
Unit 9   The political context
Unit 10 The social and economic context
Unit 11 Radical Bath
Unit 12 Electoral behaviour in Britain, 1832–68

Block four   Exercises in historical sociology
Unit 13 Social stratification
Unit 14 Social mobility
Unit 15 Family and kinship